A MODERN LOOK AT MONSTERS

A Modern Look
at Monsters

by Daniel Cohen

ILLUSTRATED

DODD, MEAD & COMPANY   NEW YORK

To Boswell and Murdoch,
two Scottish terriers who, contrary
to popular opinion, are not monsters

ACKNOWLEDGMENTS

The author is grateful to the following for aid in obtaining information or pictures for this book: James Colvin of Field Enterprises Educational, Corp., L. Sprague de Camp, Richard Dempewolff of Science Digest, Jerry Greer Fales, George Hass, Sir Edmund Hillary, Dr. Gerald P. Hodge, F.W. Holiday, David James of the Loch Ness Phenomena Investigation Bureau, John Keel, P.A. MacNab, Dr. Roy P. Mackal, Jim Mosley, Ivan T. Sanderson, Clem Skelton of LNPIB, and Paul J. Willis of the International Fortean Organization. Needless to say not all of the above would agree with the author's conclusions.

Contents

Illustrations

A MODERN LOOK AT MONSTERS

Of Men and Monsters

What is a monster?

A monster, at least as far as this book is concerned, is a possibly mythical animal, large enough or lethal enough to inspire terror. The key characteristics of a monster are, therefore, mystery and menace.

The unicorn, although it is one of history's most celebrated mythical animals, does not qualify as a monster because it does not scare people. Once, early in its history, the unicorn was regarded as a proper monster. The Roman, Julius Solinus, gave a blood-chilling description of the beast, and in the sixteenth century Arthur Golding rendered a blood-chilling translation:

"But the cruellest is the Unicorne, a monster that belloweth horrible, bodyed like a horse, footed like an elephant, tayled like a Swyne, and headed like a Stagge. His horn sticketh out of the midds of hys forehead, of a wonderful brightness about fore foote long, so sharp, that whatsoever he pusheth

1

at, he striketh it through easily. He is never caught alive, kylled he may be, but taken he cannot bee."

Later in its career, the unicorn got soft. It still couldn't be captured alive, except by a virgin. If a virgin appeared in the woods, the unicorn would come trotting out and lay its head down in her lap. There is little menace in such a creature.

A monster is usually thought of as a large animal, and most monsters are. But the basilisk, which was only a few feet long, was poisonous enough to be classed as a proper monster. The Loch Ness monster, on the other hand, is reputed to be an inoffensive, even shy creature. Yet it is large enough to send boatmen rowing in terror back to shore when they think they have spotted it.

An animal that does not make the monster class is the *martichora*, despite the fact that it:

". . . has a face like a man's, a skin red as cinnabar, and is as large as a lion. It has three rows of teeth, ears and light blue eyes like those of a man; its tail is like that of a land scorpion, containing a sting more than a cubit long at the end. It has other stings on each side of its tail and one on the top of its head, like the scorpion, with which it inflicts a wound that is always fatal. If it is attacked from a distance it sets up its tail in front and dicharges its stings as if from a bow; if attacked from behind, it straightens out and launches its stings in a direct line to the distance of a hundred feet . . ."

The *martichora* sounds like a monster but it is really a tiger as described by an early Greek who had never seen a tiger and had to rely solely on the stories brought back by travelers to India.

Oddly, a bit of that legend survives even in modern times. When I was young I recall visiting the zoo with an older friend who informed me that the lion had a poisonous claw hidden in the tuft of hair at the end of its tail. I cannot imagine how my friend had picked up that bit of misinformation. I'm sure he had never read Greek literature. The legend has probably just been kicking around in one form or another for centuries. If only the truth were half so tenacious.

Usually both the Greeks and Romans were surprisingly accurate when it came to separating the real from the unreal in the animal world. Hard-working, down-to-earth Pliny, who wrote during the first century of the Christian era, did not like to depend on hearsay. (So great was his passion for first-hand observation that in the year 79 he tried to get a close-up look at an eruption of Vesuvius, and was killed.) In his *Natural History*, Pliny wrote:

"The Pegasus with its wings and horse's head sounds very much like a legend, just as does the Gryphon in the country of the Moors. Also the Tragopan, of which many say that it is larger than an eagle, that it has curved horns and a red head, while the rest of the body is rust-colored. The Sirens should also be disbelieved . . ."

Although the Greeks and Romans did believe in many animals we now know are mythical, they were basically practical people, who put their faith in what they could see and touch. They also did a lot of traveling, the Greeks as sailors and merchants and the Romans as conquerors, so they accumulated a great body of firsthand facts upon which they could draw.

In the Middle Ages a new attitude toward nature, and a new isolation, at least for the people of Western Europe, brought forth a whole host of remarkable animals. These fabulous animals grew and flourished in a work called *Physiologus* (roughly a book by "the naturalist"). Later copies of this work were given the more appealing title of the Bestiary. The origin of *Physiologus* is unknown, but it seems to have been compiled by many writers, and begun as early as the first century of the Christian era, at about the same time Pliny wrote. While Pliny preferred to observe, these Christian writers drew heavily upon the Bible, classical authors, old legends, travelers' tales, and Lord knows what else. Bestiaries were popular for centuries and were copied, recopied, and expanded upon.

Bestiaries were essentially religious books, for all animals were assumed to have been placed on earth for man's use. (The monkey presented quite a problem, for no one could figure out what it was useful for, and the use of the mosquito was never even considered.) The animals described in the Bestiary were also supposed to illustrate lessons in Christian mystery and dogma. An early Bestiary records that the lioness gives birth to dead cubs, but on the third day the male lion enters the den and brings them to life by breathing into their their faces. This is symbolic of the Resurrection on the third day.

Were the stories in the Bestiary thought to be true? That is a hard question to answer, for one must define what the medieval Christian believed to be the meaning of truth. Saint Augustine is one supposed to have said that the important thing was "to consider the significance of a fact and not to discuss its authenticity." But most people were probably not bothered by such theological subtleties. The average man must have regarded the Bestiary as a reputable and accurate description of animal life.

Not everyone was impressed by the wonder beasts of medieval zoology. No less a personage than Saint Bernard was enraged at the ever-increasing number of fantastic animals he found adorning cathedrals and other holy places.

"What business have these ridiculous monstrosities, those amazingly freakish beauties and marvelously beautiful freaks in the cloisters right in front of the eyes of the monks who are supposed to be reading or meditating? You see one head with many bodies or one body with many heads. Here you have a serpent's tail attached to a quadruped and there a mammal's head attached to a fish's body. There you have a creature that is half horse and half goat, and here one with horns and the rear end of a horse. . . . Great God, if they do not feel shame about the nonsense they produce why don't they at least shun the expense!"

Starting with the Renaissance, people began paying closer attention to the authenticity rather than to the significance of things. By the sixteenth century a man like Konrad Gesner of Zurich was able to compile a reasonably accurate encyclopedia of the animals of the world. Naturalists began ruthlessly to purge creatures suspected of unreality from the rolls of the accepted. By 1827 the great anatomist Baron Cuvier had expelled even the ancient and much beloved unicorn, by declaring that a single-horned animal with a cloven hoof was impossible. Such an animal he noted, would have a divided frontal bone, and no horn could grow in such a spot. (The rhinoceros does not have a true horn, so does not count.)

But as the monsters were heartlessly consigned to the dustbin of myth and superstition, a small but interesting counterreformation began, and continues this day. While paying due homage to the advances in zoological knowledge over the last few centuries, the thesis of the counter-reformation is that the purging of monsters has gone too far, and that there are still many large, unknown, and truly monstrous creatures alive in the world that are not recognized by science. Today people who hold such views are called monster buffs.

A buff is a person with a passionate, almost obsessive interest in a small area of knowledge. Most familiar are certain types of sports buffs. These are the sort of people who have committed to memory the batting averages of all the players on their favorite team from the day of its founding until the current season. They can tell you without hesitating or blinking who won the third game of the World Series in 1932, and by what score. Railroad buffs are another reasonably common American phenomenon. They will travel hundreds of miles and pay an outlandish price just to spend a few hours riding on an uncomfortable old steam train.

Sports and railroads are respectable areas of interest, but there are plenty of buffs whose interests are in subjects that lay on the fringes of respectability. These are perhaps the most passionate of all. Among them are the saucer buffs, those concerned over what they consider to be an invasion of ships from outer space.

Here on the fringe must be classed the monster buffs. Indeed, many monster buffs are also saucer buffs, psychic buffs, and the like. Any fringe area seems to attract them, perhaps because it appeals to their generally anti-establishment outlook.

A sometimes not too gentle paranoia hangs over the world of the buffs. Saucer buffs see conspiracies to cover up the "truth" about the invasion from space. Monster buffs do not spend as much time looking under the bed, but they do believe that they are confronted by a conspiracy of stupidity and silence on the part of the "official scientific community." They often feel trapped and defensive.

It is this feeling that brings out some of the monster buffs' least attractive characteristics. They are much too quick to denounce their opponents as a pack of blind fools. They are also too quick to grasp at any straw which seems to support their view, and far too quick to rush into print with sensational claims for half-baked evidence. Indeed, it almost seems that to be a true monster buff one must be half romanticist and half mountebank. It is difficult to determine where one leaves off and the other begins.

At the beginning of the nineteenth century, a young French naturalist named Pierre Denys de Montfort decided the stories concerning a gigantic sea monster called the kraken, thought by most scientists to be a purely mythical beast, really described an unknown variety of "colossal octopus" which he called *poulpe colossal.* He was very nearly right, although the sea giant turned out to be the octopus' close relative the squid.

Unfortunately, Denys de Montfort uncritically published many exaggerated accounts of his *poulpe colossal* in a book he wrote on the subject. Most damning of all was a picture that he said was based on a picture found in St. Thomas' chapel in St. Malo. The picture shows a ship off the coast of Angola being attacked by a frightful squidlike monster, whose tentacles curl about the top of the ship's masts. Denys de Montfort wrote that the picture and the tradition attached to it "constituted an established fact which lies within the province of natural history which adopts all materials the fact and authenticity of which cannot be disputed."

Of course, the picture and the event were very much in dispute. There was no evidence that the attack of the giant octopus off the coast of Angola was anything more than an apocryphal sea story. It is hard to know whether the young Frenchman was really serious in presenting this tale, and many of the other disputable stories in his book. Certainly he was aware of the flimsy nature of his evidence. Later he remarked, "If my colossal octopus is accepted, I shall make it sink a whole squadron in the second edition."

He practically did this anyway when he hinted that ten ships disappeared in the West Indies on April 12, 1782, under mysterious circumstances, which in his opinion could have been caused by the attack of a gigantic cuttlefish (a close relative of the squid and octopus). Unfortunately, this time Denys de Montfort's facts simply did not square away with those of the British Admiralty, and his reputation sank deeper than his missing ships. He unsuccessfully tried a number of occupations, and according to one account finally turned to a life of crime and died in prison. The real circumstances of his death were less dramatic. Reduced to pauperism, he was found "dead and destitute in a Paris street in 1820 or 1821." He was fifty-six years old.

What manner of man was Denys de Montfort? Many believe, because of his remark about having the giant octopus overthrow a fleet in the second edition, that he was a cavalier charlatan. His supporters, however, contend that he was a man of great foresight, and that such remarks were bitter jokes with which he responded to the slings and arrows of a hostile and obstinate scientific community.

The story of Constantin Samuel Rafinesque-Schmaltz has some striking parallels to that of Denys de Montfort. Rafinesque was a French-American naturalist who enthusiastically supported the existence of the great sea serpent. It is hard to say whether the sea serpent hurt Rafinesque's reputation or vice versa. By 1817 when Rafinesque published his first dissertation on sea serpents he was already a well-known character. Highly eccentric in his habits and appearance, Rafinesque was accustomed to quarreling violently with anyone who disagreed with him, and that was practically everyone.

After one particularly violent quarrel Rafinesque was thrown out of his job at the University of Lexington, and like Denys de Montfort died in wretched poverty at the age of fifty-six.

In modern times, another romantic and supporter of monsters, the Belgian-French naturalist Bernard Heuvelmans, dedicated his tome on sea serpents "To the memory of those two ill-fated naturalists, Pierre Denys de Montfort and Constantin Samuel Rafinesque and to all those who in perfectly good faith have bravely reported facts not easy to believe." The brotherhood of persecuted prophets spans the centuries.

Another feature of many monster buffs is their anti-intellectualism. The buffs often celebrate the hairy-chested adventurer, the plain, straight-talking ordinary guy, the great rugged individualist, that fellow so beloved in American folklore, and so rare as to probably be mythical himself.

This imaginary common-man adventurer is set up in opposition to his arch enemy, the equally mythical stuffed-shirt scientist. You know the stereotype, the guy with the chalk on his coat and funny hair, who hasn't poked his nose outside of a university for thirty years. In fact, many of the scientists so scorned by the buffs have spent years in the field, and very little time behind a desk, while the buffs themselves often experience the outdoors only during the hunting season, and then for as brief a period as possible. But the theme of outdoorsman versus scientist runs through many modern monster stories, and it is, I suspect, one of the reasons for the popularity of monster stories in many of the "huntin' and fishin'" type of magazine.

Feeling persecuted by the "establishment" and also wishing to remain free of the often oppressive restrictions of scientific proof, the buff seems prone to falling into a state of mind where he genuinely cannot distinguish truth from publicity. Like Denys de Montfort, the modern monster buff often seems to support the most extravagant and improbable of stories, stories that he should easily be able to see through. Is he lying? Putting us on? Or is he blinded by faith and the desire to further "the cause"? I suspect the latter, but that strange mixture of true believer and mountebank sometimes makes one wonder if there is not a smile behind all those protestations of sincerity.

While this mixture of characteristics can make the monster buff irritating, it can also make him uniquely attractive. In our difficult world there is something wildly, deliciously, almost sinfully irresponsible about a fellow who really gets worked up over the Loch Ness monster.

One feels a bit like a fourteenth-century peasant, who

might take a brief respite from his humdrum labor to go the fair and listen to an exotic stranger speak of the griffin and the roc and the other monstrous creatures of "the Uttermost East."

Monster buffery, therefore, is escapism, pure and simple. So long as it does not go too far, to the point where one sees the monsters regularly popping out of the woods (an unfortunate extreme that does overtake a few of the buffs), it can be a useful and stimulating exercise of the mind and the imagination.

II

The Birth of Monsters

When Hernán Cortés invaded Mexico he had fifteen cavalry men under his command. This handful of mounted men had an effect far exceeding their limited number. The Aztecs, who had never seen a horse before, much less a man on horseback, were terrified. They thought that man and horse were one.

The Incas of Peru reacted even more violently to Pizarro's horsemen. When one of the riders fell from his horse, the Inca warriors fled in panic, thinking that somehow the monster had broken in two.

William Prescott, who wrote the classic history of the conquest of Latin America, drew the analogy between the first impressions of the Aztecs and Incas upon seeing a man on horseback and the centaur, the half-man, half-horse monster of Greek mythology. Unlike the Indians, the early Europeans knew horses or at least horselike creatures. Early civilizations had used horse-drawn wagons, and somewhat later the horse-drawn war chariot became a standard part of the equipment of armies throughout the Middle East and North Africa. But riding was a comparatively late introduction in the civilized world.

The first riders that civilized peoples of the Middle East saw were probably nomadic tribesmen who swept out of the Eurasian steppe as robbers and invaders. Riding almost certainly developed on the steppe, and the nomads were traditionally superb horsemen. Even later invaders like the Huns continued to inspire an almost supernatural terror among the peoples of the Roman world. Roman writers mentioned again and again how Hunnish rider and horse seemed to be one. It is not hard to imagine that those civilized city dwellers who faced the first invasion of mounted men reacted exactly the same way that the Aztecs and Incas had: they believed that horse and rider were one. And thus began the legend of the centaur. In Greek mythology centaurs were described as fierce, wild, and tribal—words which could well apply to the nomadic horsemen.

It is comforting to begin a search for the origins of ancient monster legends with this story of the centaur. If only one could speak with such easy assurance about the origins of the other monsters. A search for the beginning of the stories of the griffin (or gryphon), that fearsome half lion, half eagle, is typically tangled. Most of us probably became acquainted with the griffin through *Alice in Wonderland:* "They very soon came upon a Gryphon, lying asleep in the sun. (If you don't know what a Gryphon is, look at the picture) . . . Alice did not quite like the look of the creature . . ." As it turned out Lewis Carroll's griffin was a harmless even vapid creature. This, however, was far from typical of griffins. A medieval Bestiary warns men to stay away from the griffin "because it feasts upon them at any opportunity." The warning continues: "It is also extremely fond of eating horses."

Some people have suggested that, despite its frequent mention in literature, the griffin was never seriously believed to be a real animal. The griffin, they say, owes its origin to a heraldic practice called dimidiation. When two noble families were joined in marriage the elements that had dominated the coat of arms of each side were combined into a new design. Thus, the family of the eagle might at some point have married into the family of the lion, and the result was a hybrid, the griffin, which adorned the new coat of arms. The griffin was a common creature of heraldry.

This solution, though theoretical, is attractive but for one small detail—the griffin is far older than the practice of heraldry. One medieval Bestiary speaks of the griffin as living mostly in "high mountains or in Hyperborean lands"—that is somewhere to the far north. The Romans had heard rumors of griffins in Central Asia. The depredations of these wild creatures were cited by refugees who came to Rome from the East as one of the major reasons for the mass movement of barbarian peoples which ultimately brought down the Roman Empire. The griffin was also a common element in the art of the nomadic Scythians of the steppe, and it seems likely that they picked it up from peoples to the north and east.

But the griffin was not associated solely with the northland. Pliny wrote of "the Gryphon in the country of the Moors." Pliny, you will recall, did not believe that such a monster existed.

Throughout the Middle Ages, objects reputed to be "griffin's claws" were brought to the markets of Europe. Those that came from the north were usually the tusks of extinct mammoths or the horns of the equally extinct woolly rhinoceros. Those "griffin's claws" from the southern regions were most often the horns of antelopes.

The griffin is not unique in the animal mythology of the world. A variety of fierce mammal birds play an important role in the legends of many parts of the Middle East and India. The Persian *senmurv* or *sinamru* (perhaps "dog-bird"), while terrible in appearance and power, was thought to be a protector of mankind. The *garuda* of India is also benevolent. This deity is part bird and part man and closely associated with the god Vishnu. In Japan there was the troublesome *tengu,* a part-bird, part-man creature. In China the *T'ien Kou* or Heaven Dog was more terrifying than troublesome. It was an omen of evil often associated with comets and other frightening meteorological phenomena.

Are these various Oriental mammal-birds ancestral to the griffin? It is hard to say, for the family tree is not at all clear, but it seems reasonable to suspect that all of these various mythological conceptions developed in response to the same sort of creature in the natural world—the eagle or some other large bird of prey. The eagle might indeed seem fierce as a lion when compared with the other birds. Perhaps thousands of years ago men described the eagle or hawk as a "lionlike bird" or even a "lion bird." What began as a descriptive phrase might have been transformed by the artist into a hybrid which combined features of both eagle and lion. Ultimately the origins of this hybrid would be lost and the griffin, half lion and half eagle, would be enshrined in medieval bestiaries as a real animal that lived in a distant land. This myth would be reinforced by the occasional appearance of griffin's claws on the market. In addition there were doubtless tales told by travelers who said they had actually seen the monster firsthand, or had at least talked to people who had seen it firsthand.

While on the subject of bird monsters, we might have a look at the origins of that giant among fabulous birds, the roc. The roc is best known to us from the tales of the voyages of Es-Sindibad, or Sindbad the Sailor. Sindbad's adventures were related in *A Thousand and One Nights,* a collection of ancient tales from the Middle East.

The size of the roc is expressed in nothing but superlatives. When Sindbad first saw the roc's egg he thought it was the dome of a great building. Then the sky darkened and Sindbad saw "a bird of enormous size, bulky body, and wide wings, flying in the air; and this it was that concealed the body of the sun, and veiled it from view." The roc, says the story, fed elephants to its young. When Sindbad angered a roc, the giant bird took its revenge by dropping stones on his ships and sinking one.

If ever there was a purely imaginary monster, the roc sounds like it. Yet there are hints that the roc was more than a legend. Marco Polo mentions the roc, and says that the Great Khan of Cathay asked for evidence of the creature. An envoy brought back to the khan a gigantic feather from the island that was supposed to be the roc's home. The khan was impressed.

Marco indicates that the island home of the roc was Madagascar, and Madagascar was the home of a really gigantic bird. The bird is called *Aepyornis maximus,* or the elephant bird. It looked like a big ostrich and may have been the largest bird that ever lived. But more impressive than the size of the bird itself was the size of its eggs. They had the capacity of six ostrich eggs or 148 chicken eggs.

While *Aepyornis maximus* is definitely no longer with us, the time of its extinction is not known with any certainty. The elephant bird may very well have survived into the sixteenth century, and its extinction was probably brought about by hunters who preyed both on the huge birds and on their eggs. The trip from Madagascar to Baghdad, the city of *A Thousand and One Nights,* is a long one, but medieval Arabs were great sailors and traders. They conducted a thriving trade along the east coast of Africa, before the trade was disrupted by the Portuguese in the fifteenth and sixteenth centuries. Arab traders undoubtedly visited Madagascar, and they might have seen living specimens of *Aepyornis maximus*. Large numbers of broken eggshells of the giant bird have been found along the coast, and this has given rise to the theory that the Arab sailors themselves helped kill off the birds by stealing eggs for food and for use as convenient cups for holding liquid. Such monstrous eggshells would also have been valuable trade items and curious souvenirs to bring back to show the family and friends.

These same Arab merchants traveled as far as China and carried the tale of the roc with them to the court of the Great Khan. The "feather" shown at the khan's court could have been the frond of *sagus ruffia*, a palm tree that grows on Madagascar. This particular palm has enormous fronds. The general similarity of shape of the palm frond and a feather would not have escaped the notice of canny merchants anxious to impress the rich khan with the wonders of the Africa trade.

But the roc cannot be explained so simply, for our roc is really the *rukh*, a huge bird that figured prominently in ancient Indian mythology. Perhaps it would be more accurate to say that *A Thousand and One Nights* is really based on traditional tales of the Middle East and India, some of which date back to the third or fourth millennium B.C. Therefore the legend of the roc was around a long time before anyone in the Middle East could have gotten to Madagascar to catch sight of *Aepyornis maximus*. And there are other problems with this identification. The roc is definitely a flying bird, yet *Aepyornis maximus*, like the ostrich, was flightless. Its size might well have inspired legends of giants, but not flying giants.

For the origins of the roc-rukh legends we must again turn to the eagle or other large birds of prey. These creatures seem to have played an extremely important part in the mythology of the Middle East from earliest times. Eagle-like figures pop up in the art of the Sumerians, the earliest-known civilization. After centuries of retelling, one branch of the legendary cycle that surrounded the eagle must have grown into the legends of the huge rukh. When Arab traders returned from Madagascar with tales of enormous eggs, or with the eggshells themselves, this doubtless strengthened the legend of the rukh. People could no longer doubt its existence simply because they had never seen it. With their own eyes they beheld the shells of eggs that could not have been laid by any ordinary bird. Naturally the eggs were nowhere near the size of the one described in the Sindbad tales, but those stories were avowedly fiction, and the storyteller's exaggeration was taken for granted.

Few had seen the roc alive because these monstrous birds lived in a distant island that was very hard to get to. No doubt more than one latter-day Sindbad spiced up his reminiscences of past voyages with descriptions of the roc that he was supposed to have seen. Who could dispute such a story? All of these—traditions, misinterpretations, misleading evidence, and deliberate falsehoods—converged to make the tale of the monster bird, the roc.

I suspect that most monster legends grew in a manner similar to those of the griffin and the roc. They started with observations of a real creature. These observations then became exaggerated and twisted through constant retelling, until the animal with which they had orinigally been associated was forgotten completely. The next step was to place this legendary animal in some distant or otherwise hard-to-reach place to explain why it was not seen more frequently. Bits of evidence like the griffin's claws or the roc's eggs were brought back to support the legend, and so it continued to flourish.

Travelers' tales added an additional flavor of authenticity to the story.

From the seventeenth to the nineteenth centuries, when monsters were being purged from the lists of "accepted" animals, many were declared to be purely imaginary in origin— the products of ignorance and superstition. Natural scientists were understandably anxious to rid their field of study of winged horses and nine-headed hydras. But they often failed to recognize that even superstitions must start somewhere.

Yet one must admit that there are some monsters which seem to have no beginning in nature at all. Perhaps these tales began so long ago and have been so altered in the re-telling that the origins are no longer recoverable. The one creature that seems most likely to have started only in man's imagination is the chimera. The name itself today has come to mean imaginary and unreal. She—for there could be only one chimera at a time, and it seems to have been a female—was described as having the head of a lion, the body of a goat, and the tail of a serpent. Sometimes she is shown as actually having a goat's head growing out of the middle of her back. For good measure she could breathe fire. The chimera, according to Greek mythology, is supposed to have lived in Asia Minor, and the Greeks probably picked up the idea of this monster, though in a much altered form, from some Oriental myth. So it is possible that even the chimera herself originated with some sort of real animal, though which of its three parts was the original is impossible to say.

The sphinx, one of the most persistent monsters of the ancient world, is also probably imaginary. Unlike the chimera, however, the sphinx is definitely bisexual. The Egyptian sphinx has a lion's body with a man's head, while the Greek sphinx has a lion's body with a woman's head and breasts. There is a difference in personality, too. The male Egyptian sphinx was reputed to be a benevolent protector, especially of the dead. The female Grecian sphinx on the other hand had a nasty reputation of ripping to pieces people who could not answer her riddles. Actually both sphinxes had a reputation for being enigmatic.

The sphinx is the most famous of the huge host of part-human, part-animal creatures that can be found in the mythology and religion of practically every society throughout history, from the nameless hybrids of the Sumerians, to Anabus the jackal-headed god of Egypt, to Ganesha the elephant-headed god of India, to the many totem figures of the American Indians. Many explanations have been offered for the universal obsession with man-animal hybrids. I would like to present one, not wholly original, that seems to me to be the most simple and straightforward.

The earliest artists that we know of, those who painted pictures deep inside limestone caves in France and Spain, were essentially realistic and practical. There are no monsters in cave art. The artists drew animals that their fellow tribesmen hunted. Often these animals were shown pierced with arrows or trapped in pits. The artists were probably attempting to perform a ritual of sympathetic magic. If the scene of the buffalo brought down by hunters' spears was painted on a cave wall, then by the magical principle of like produces like, the scene should be re-enacted when the hunt actually took place.

The same principle of sympathetic magic was probably used in other ceremonies, for example, tribal dances. Here man dressed in animal skins would act out the hunt scene. Men shown dressed in animal costumes are depicted in several pieces of cave art. Animal disguises played an important part in the ceremonies, and even in the actual hunting practices of the North American Indians. (Before the introduction of the horse, Indians would sneak up on buffalo herds, disguised as buffalo.)

After a time the masquerader would take on a life and power of his own. A belief in sympathetic magic decrees that if a man wears an animal skin or other animal disguise, then he should be able to absorb some of the qualities of that animal. From a substitute animal, the masquerader became a magical person, a god, and occasionally a monster.

Many commentators have attempted to explain the existence of monsters in the mythology of the world by probing the psyche of primitive man. Monsters, according to this way of thinking, are symbols drawn from the dark recesses of the mind. They are symbols of night, death, sex, or whatever. In our psychologically oriented society such theorizing has been popular, but we must recognize that there is no evidence to support it. We do not know how primitive man thought; the only glimpse we get—the art of the cave men—shows no monsters. Modern-day "primitives" such as the Australian aborigine and the Indians of the Amazon jungle do not help us, for such peoples are only technologically primitive. Their cultures and beliefs are ancient and complex, for they have been human as long as we have. (Modern "primitives" are usually peoples who have fallen from a more developed state of social organization, rather than peoples who have not advanced.) Only with civilization do monsters seem to play a significant role. The art of the Sumerians and to a lesser extent that of the Egyptians is filled with strange and unreal beasts.

Certainly not all man-animal monsters can be explained as the result of ritual masquerade. The centaur we have already shown has quite a different origin. But certainly the animal-headed gods of Egypt look very much like ordinary men wearing animal masks. The point here is that these creatures were probably not the products of an unconnected imagination—they were born out of real experience. People believed in Anabus, the jackal-headed god, because somewhere in the past people had seen a man in a jackal mask.

Although monsters were rarely invented out of whole cloth, some may have begun with something as humble as a mistranslation. Take the tangled history of the basilisk or cocktrace. The basilisk is first described as an extremely poisonous snake. Old Pliny described the basilisk as a snake with a crown upon its head. "It destroys all shrubs, not only by its contact, but those that it has breathed upon; it burns up all the grass too, and breaks the stones, so tremendous is its noxious influence. It was formerly a general belief that if a man on horseback killed one of these animals with a spear, the poison would run up the weapon and kill, not only the rider, but the horse as well. To this dreadful monster the effluvium of the weasel is fatal . . . it has pleased nature that there should be nothing without its antidote." What snake inspired this terrifying story we do not know. There is a type of grass snake that has two crescent-shaped bright yellow patches at the back of its head. These are, even today, ofen called a crown. The name basilisk itself means "king of all snakes," since the Greek word for king is *basileus*.

Both Greeks and Romans accepted the basilisk as an unusually venomous snake. Various Old Testament references to adders or serpents were from time to time mistranslated as basilisk. By the Middle Ages the idea of the basilisk was widely accepted throughout Europe, for its existence was confirmed both by classical authors and the Bible. Medieval writers did little original research or thinking—they merely consulted the standard works. But during the late Middle Ages this "king of all snakes" began to acquire more than just a crown. While remaining essentially a serpent, the basilisk was also believed to have some of the characteristics of a cock and of a toad. In view of the circumstances of its birth this mixture of characteristics is unsurprising. The basilisk, it was said, was hatched from an egg laid by a seven-year-old cock during the days of the dog star Sirius. This egg was incubated by either a toad or the cock itself (there was some dispute on this point). Naturally basilisks were quite rare, and a good thing too, for the breath of one or even its glance was deadly. Powder made from the ashes of a basilisk was used in alchemical experiments, which is perhaps why the alchemists never succeeded.

Just how a simple, though highly poisonous serpent acquired such a shape, we do not really know. Perhaps here the heraldic practice of dimidiation had a part to play.

In the Middle Ages, basilisks were blamed for all sorts of things. If a cellar mysteriously became filled with noxious fumes, then a basilisk must be responsible. If the water in a well became polluted and the cause was unknown, then it was assumed that a basilisk was in the vicinity.

Though the legend of the basilisk remained popular some natural scientists tried to refute it. In the sixteenth century Konrad Gesner condemned this monster as "Woman's gossip and false nonsense." Yet the common people, then as now, refused to accept the world of experts.

In 1587 there was a big basilisk hunt in Warsaw. It was perhaps the last basilisk hunt the world has seen. Two small girls had been found dead in a cellar and it was assumed, for what reason we do not know, that they had been killed by a basilisk. The people of Warsaw looked for a brave champion who would go into the cellar and dispatch the poisonous monster. But none was found, and the only "volunteer" was a criminal who was already under sentence of death.

Thousands gathered to watch the condemned man, fitted out in a traditional basilisk hunting costume, a leather suit covered with mirrors (mirrors were excellent protection against basilisks for the monster's glance was fatal, even to itself), descend into the cellar. After an almost unbearably long time the man emerged carrying what looked like an ordinary snake. But the king's own physician declared it to be a basilisk. Who would disagree?

At about this same time, the remains of dried or otherwise preserved basilisks began appearing in collections of natural curiosities throughout Europe. These basilisks were really manufactured monsters called Jenny Hanivers. (The origin of the odd and interesting name Jenny Haniver is unknown.)

The basic Jenny Haniver was usually a skate or ray, flattened relatives of the shark. These creatures could be cut and fashioned in various rather startling ways. The result was often a creation that looked as though it had the body and wings of some sort of bird and the tail of a lizard or snake.

In nature, the face of the ray has a vaguely human appearance. It was this that probably first gave fishermen the idea of making fake monsters. With a little help the ray's "face" can be cut and pulled into something that could only be the face of a monster. So common were Jenny Hanivers that, according to Willy Ley, "there is no doubt that these Jenny Hanivers greatly influenced the popular conception of the appearance of the basilisk."

Although Gesner and all other natural scientists of that time and after knew about Jenny Hanivers, and specifically warned against them, the fake monsters continued to find their way into collections. They also continued to be produced as proof of the truth of the legend of the basilisk and, as we shall see, of the legend of the dragon as well.

A creature that probably owes its entire existence to Jenny Hanivers is the sea monk and its ecclesiastical superior the sea bishop. These creatures were fairly small and generally inoffensive, hardly monsters at all, although they were reputed to have the ability to whip up storms. The two creatures were described most fully in *Books of Sea Fishes* by Guilielmus Rondeletius, published in 1554. The sea monk had a human face and tonsured head, fins and a rather fishy tail. The sea bishop had legs rather than a tail and, of course, wore a miter.

Neither of these creatures is of great antiquity, and the stories about them, for example, the one in which a sea bishop visits the court of Poland in 1531, are obvious fairy tales. Pictures published by Rondeletius show that both creatures could have been manufactured from skates or rays with perhaps pieces of other sea creatures sewed on.

Whether the Jenny Hanivers stimulated the stories, or the stories inspired the Jenny Hanivers, we do not know. But there is evidence to suggest that the Jenny Hanivers came first. As late as 1933 fishermen who had never heard of basilisks or sea monks were manufacturing Jenny Hanivers in the United States because they had been struck by the resemblance between the face of a ray or skate and a human face. In 1969 a photo of an obvious Jenny Haniver was distributed by a national photo service as a picture of a genuine sea creature.

More monstrous in both size and power is the Chinese version of the sea monk, the sea bonze (Buddhist priest of the sea, or *Hai Ho Shang*). This monster was big enough to capsize boats and evil-tempered enough to do so on every possible occasion. Chinese sailors performed various rituals, including burning feathers on deck, to keep the *Hai Ho Shang* away.

The dugong, seal, and giant ray or devilfish have all been suggested as the creatures that inspired the legend of the *Hai Ho Shang*, but there simply is not enough known about the subject to draw even a tentative conclusion.

Mermaids, and their male counterparts, mermen, are generally harmless (although like sirens, the mermaids could call sailors to their death). Still it is hard to class them as monsters, and their history has been adequately traced by others.

There is, however, one lesser-known species of mermen, the *homen marinho*, that lived on the coast of South America and had some pretty monstrous habits, so it deserves mention.

These monsters were supposed to be more or less human in appearance, but more dangerous and malignant than the shark. They lived by the water and strangled anyone they happened to catch. Often they ate their victims. The *homen marinho* was reported quite soberly by two apparently reliable observers, the Jesuit Father Fernão Cardium and sugar planter Gabriel Soares. One suspects that this legend began when one or more bands of shipwrecked sailors were reduced to robbery and cannibalism in order to survive.

The hydra is yet another ancient monster of the sea that probably did not originate solely in our subconscious. In Geek legend the hydra was a nine-headed monster that lived in a swamp. Each time one of its heads was cut off a new one would grow in its place. The monster was finally defeated by Hercules who burned off eight of the heads and buried the ninth, the immortal center head, under a stone.

Most naturalists feel fairly certain that the creature that inspired the hydra of mythology was the octopus. The eight tentacles became heads in the legend, and the creatures' real head became the ninth immortal head of the legendary monster. The octopus does have the ability to regenerate lost tentacles—hence the mythical hydra's ability to regenerate lost heads. Homer's many-headed Scylla, the monster that nearly finished Ulysses, may also have been an octopus, although the reference is less clear.

The strength and ferocity of the octopus have been so much exaggerated that many have accepted the equally false belief that an octopus can't be dangerous at all. The octopus of the Mediterranean, the one that would have been encountered by the Greeks, can grow to a diameter of ten feet. (The North Atlantic octopus gets even larger, attaining a diameter of over twenty-five feet, but it is hard to see how these could have figured in the hydra myth.) A large octopus has a great deal of power in its arms and suckers, and more than one man has probably been dragged to his death by a large octopus. Besides, the mere appearance of an octopus would inspire terror in most people even if the octopus were entirely harmless. It is the kind of animal around which legends grow.

A thirteenth-century writer, Conrad von Megenberg, had another explanation for the legendary hydra:

"Some say that Hydra is a dragon with many heads and that one of this kind lived in a swamp near Lerna in Arcadia. The storytellers say that it grew three heads for each head that was severed. But this is not true . . . The area was rich with flowing water and the waters were so powerful and so wild that they ruined the city. If one spring was dammed up, three or four others came up elsewhere. This was seen by the hero Herakles who brought much soil and heavy stones and filled in the whole swamp, making it dry. A man of ill will acts just like the Hydra, if you punish him for having done some evil he will commit four new misdeeds for the one that was forbidden."

Finally let us turn to the kraken, that monster most beloved by all monster buffs since it is one monster that turned out really to exist. This particular monster is not of great antiquity. It is mentioned first in the book *A Natural History of Norway* published in 1752–1753 and written by Erik Ludvigsen Pontoppidan, Bishop of Bergen, Pontoppidan writes of what is "incontestably the largest Sea-monster in the world . . . It is called Kraken, Kraxen, or some name it Krabben, that word being applied by way of eminences to this creature. This last name seems indeed best to agree with the description of this creature, which is round, flat, and full of arms, or branches. Others call it also *Horven,* or *Söe-horven,* and some *Anker-trold.*"

From the above description and others given by Pontoppidan it is not difficult to see that the creature he is talking
about is almost certainly the giant squid. Pontoppidan himself believed, "This enormous Sea-animal in all probability
may be reckon'd of the Polyp, or of the Starfish kind." Actually the squid is a mollusk, but Pontoppidan had correctly
guessed the invertebrate nature of the monster.

Earlier, in 1555, Olaus Magnus, another Scandinavian
bishop, had apparently heard of the giant squid, but he could
not imagine such a large sea creature unless it were a fish, so
he called it a "monstrous fish" and described it thus:

"Their Forms are horrible, their Heads square, all set with
prickles, and they have sharp and long Horns round about,
like a Tree rooted up by the Roots: They are [about twenty
feet] long, very black, and with huge eyes . . . the Apple of
the eye is [two feet]. . . ."

Although a picture of the creature in Olaus' book makes it
look like a prickly and bearded fish, there is no doubt that
this "monstrous fish" is also a squid for a squid with its
tentacles looks extraordinarily like "a Tree rooted up by the
Roots," and mention of the creature's eye is also significant
for squids do have large and very prominent eyes.

What made Pontoppidan's kraken so difficult to believe in
was the utterly fantastic size he attributed to the thing:

"Its back or upper part, which seems to be in appearance
about an English mile and a half in circumference (some say
more, but I chose the least for greater certainty), looks at
first like a number of small islands, surrounded by something
that floats and fluctuates like sea weed."

Pontoppidan notes that the kraken's arms or tentacles are
so huge that they could easily pull down the largest man-of-
war but "The Kraken has never been known to do any great
harm, except that they have taken away the lives of those
who consequently could not bring back the tidings." One

would hardly be enthusiastic about encountering the kraken after a recommendation like that.

Another detail of the kraken legend, which Pontoppidan did not believe in, was that there were only two of these giants and that they were almost immortal, coming to the surface to die only when the world was to end. Pontoppidan mentions a kraken, "perhaps a young and careless one," which became trapped among the rocks at Fredrikstad. The stench of its rotting carcass made passing the narrow channel most unpleasant.

The squid was well known even in Pontoppidan's day; what people did not know was how large squids could grow. The largest known squid was only a few feet long, and that length included the tube-shaped body, eight arms or tentacles, and the two elongated tentacles which often accounted for nearly half the squid's length. In fact, even today, we don't really know how large the giant squid can grow. Upper limits are seriously quoted at anywhere from seventy to over two hundred feet.

The giant squid is a creature of the depths; it does not seem to come to the surface unless it is sick or otherwise disturbed. The only measurements that biologists can obtain are from those occasional specimens washed ashore. This is not very satisfactory, since the creatures rot rather quickly and have often partially decomposed before anyone ever got around to measuring them. Besides, there is no particular reason to believe that the largest of these deep sea giants ever do get washed ashore at all.

But at least we now know that there is such a thing as a giant squid, and that whatever the upper limits of its growth, it is far and away he largest known invertebrate and also the major source for the kraken legend. I say major source, for the legend of the kraken seems to have intermingled with the legend of the island beast that was current during the early Middle Ages. The island beast was another enormous sea creature that spent a good deal of time floating quietly around on the surface of the ocean. Its featureless back was sometimes mistaken for an island by sailors, and occasionally these sailors would go "ashore" and build a fire to cook their dinners, and then . . . well, one wonders how they got back to tell the tale.

The island beast was probably a large whale of some sort, for the giant squid, as far as we know, does not spend a great deal of time floating around on the surface. Being a gill breather it does not have to come to the surface at all, as the whale does. Indeed, it was the giant squid's deep-sea habits that kept it unknown for so long. Besides, the squid has a characteristic reddish color and looks far less islandlike than the dark back of a whale. Pontoppidan describes an emerging kraken as looking like "a number of small islands." Could these islands have been in reality a herd of whales basking on the surface? Others have suggested that the islands were a herd of giant squids, but since one squid is unlikely to be basking on the surface, it is even less likely that a herd of them would do so, unless they had been driven up by undersea conditions about which we presently know nothing.

Certainly even the occasional appearance of a giant squid on the surface would have been quite impressive and frightening enough to make a very deep and lasting impression on the mind of any mariner. Even the most experienced might well be led to exaggerate the creature's size and to identify anything large and not immediately recognizable as something else, as the kraken.

Just how long the kraken remained in the shadow world, regarded as an unknown monster to be ridiculed by scientists and feared by sailors, is hard to say. Denys de Montfort began his disastrous campaign for recognition of the creature around the turn of the nineteenth century. A half century later a Danish zoologist, Johan Japetus Seenstrup, published a description of the giant squid and even gave it the scientific name *Architeuthis monachus*. This act may not have met the universal approval of Steenstrup's colleagues, but it did not meet universal derision either. You could say that 1857 was the year that science "accepted" the kraken, although much reduced in size, as the giant squid. Thus it had remained "unknown" for about a century, from the time of Pontoppidan's published description until Steenstrup's naming.

A few years later, in 1861, the French sloop *Alecton* actually harpooned a huge squid, and in a letter to the Minister of the Navy the commander of the *Alecton* describes the creatures as "the giant calamary" (squid). At about this point the remains of huge squids washed up on beaches throughout the world began to be reported with more accuracy. Scientists realized that for centuries many fishermen had been so blasé about giant squids that they had been cutting up the carcasses and using them for bait.

If any more evidence were needed for the existence of giant squids, it can be found in the form of round scars occasionally marring the backs and sides of sperm whales. These scars were made by the suckers on the tentacles of huge squids. Sperm whales normally feed on squids, but the giant variety is more than even a whale can swallow. If a sperm whale mistakenly happened to attack a giant squid, you can be quite sure the monster would fight back.

In 1875 the men aboard the barque *Pauline* witnessed what appeared to them to be a death struggle between a sea serpent and a sperm whale. Many authorities now believe that what they actually saw was the tentacles of a huge squid coiled about a sperm whale. Although the giant squid was "accepted" by science in 1875, its existence was certainly not well known. After a struggle of about fifteen minutes, the *Pauline* reported the whale seemed to be picked up in the air and then dragged downward by the victorious monster.

Perhaps the kraken is not "incontestably the largest Sea-Monster in the world" as Bishop Pontoppidan thought it was, but if the interpretation of the *Pauline* sighting is correct, then the squid can be quite large and monstrous enough to satisfy most tastes—for what other creature is there that can throw a whale around?

III

The Greatest Monster of Them All

In 1969 the Roman Catholic Church announced sweeping reforms in its liturgical calendar. Among them, Vatican authorities expressed serious doubts as to whether a number of popular saints who had been venerated for centuries ever existed at all. Among the disputed were Saint Christopher, patron saint of travelers, and Saint Nicholas and Saint Valentine, patron saints of major holidays. But the saint who concerns us here is the patron saint of England and the most famous dragon killer of all times, Saint George.

How did the tale of the doubtful saint and the dubious monster ever begin? Is it even possible that the dragon is going to have the last laugh by turning out to be more real than Saint George?

The origins of the story of Saint George and the dragon are obscure. Here is the story, as it is generally believed to have begun: Saint George was a Christian from Palestine who served in the Roman army during the early years of the fourth century. With the legions he traveled to many places as a loyal soldier of the emperor. Somewhere during his travels he met and defeated a dragon in battle. This act has become the most famous of his career. Saint George is rarely represented without a lance in his hand and a mortally wounded dragon beneath his feet. But it was not besting the monster that gave George his sainthood. The reigning emperor at the time George served in the Roman army was Diocletian. He had started with a tolerant attitude toward Christianity, but later in his reign he turned bitterly against it. After the emperor's change, George resigned from the army and openly denounced Diocletian's anti-Christian edicts. For such impertinence the soldier was arrested, tortured, and finally executed, becoming one of many Christian martyrs at the end of Diocletian's reign. Tradition set the day of Saint George's death as April 23, 303, and April 23 was celebrated as Saint George's feast day until the recent change in the liturgical calendar.

After his death the body of the martyr was supposed to have been returned to his birthplace in Lydda for burial. It is Lydda that provides the key to the legend of Saint George and the dragon. In the district of Lydda is Jaffa or Joppa. Off the shore of this seaport town is a rock that, according to ancient classical tradition, was the very rock upon which the maid Andromeda was chained and exposed to the ravages of the sea monster. Andromeda had offended the god Poseidon, and Greek gods were notoriously touchy about their honor.

Andromeda was saved from the monster by the hero Perseus, who just happened to be passing by. The hero instantly fell in love with Andromeda and slew the monster that was threatening her. The story of Andromeda and the sea monster doubtless predates the Greeks, but its true origins are lost.

After the triumph of Christianity, a Christian hero from

the general vicinity of the monster slaying appropriated the attributes of the earlier pagan hero. The sea monster gave way to a more celebrated monster, the dragon.

Saint George became one of the most popular saints of the Eastern Church. When the Crusaders entered the Holy Land they picked up the enthusiasm for this military martyr and carried it back to Europe. By the fourteenth century Saint George had been proclaimed the official saint of England.

The English were not content to admire Saint George from afar. The stories of his travels were embroidered, until one of them had him visiting Britain, which in the time of Diocletian was a distant province of the Roman empire. It was in Britain, said the British, that Saint George had his fateful encounter with the dragon. They could even show you where the battle took place, Dragon's Hill in Berkshire. A bare spot on the hill was where the slain monster's blood flowed out, making it impossible for anything to grow there. A hill in England is a long way from a rock off the coast of Palestine.

In the story of Saint George and the dragon we get a glimpse of the complexities we encounter when we try to probe the history of the dragon. The dragon is without doubt the number one monster of all times.

In Christianity the dragon is the embodiment of evil, closely identified with Satan and the Antichrist. It is evil in the form of a dragon that is cast out of heaven by the Archangel Michael: "And the great dragon was cast out, that old serpent, called the Devil, and Satan, which deceiveth the whole world: he was cast out into the earth, and his angels were cast out with him" (Rev. 12:9).

But to the medieval Christian the dragon was not merely an allegorical personification of evil, it was a very real animal, as real as the lion or the rhinoceros. Well into the seventeenth century learned men wrote learned accounts of the habits and appearances of dragons. Dragons were classified in books of natural history as one might classify different kinds of dogs or birds.

What sets the dragon above all other monsters, however, is the universality of belief in it. Not only is the dragon pre-eminent in the mythology of Christian Europe, it is also the premier mythological animal of the Orient as well. Among the folklore of peoples of Africa and pre-Columbian North and South America there can be found many dragonlike creatures.

Although they look rather alike, the Western dragon is a symbol of Satan and evil, while the Oriental dragon is a symbol of royal power, and is usually quite benevolent. The contrast between Eastern and Western dragons is so striking that the two types must be considered separately. Let us start with the Western dragon.

Attempts to explain the origin of the dragon myth in the West have been numerous, and not very successful. In his book *Fabulous Beasts* Peter Lum writes: "He [the dragon] was already old when the first myths of which we have any record were developing, and it is thought possible that the curse laid on the serpent in the Old Testament was an attempt to discredit a powerful dragon-serpent cult that was flourishing when the Jewish religion was first formulated. It has even been suggested that horror inspired in Europe and the Near East by the dragon reflects a time of which we have no record, a time when the white race was engaged in a terrific struggle for survival against the black race, who until then had been masters of the world and whose emblem was the dragon."

There is not a scrap of proof to support either of these theories. Indeed, the theory of the struggle between the white race and the dragon-emblazoned black race can be disregarded as a bit of racist nonsense. It would be far more logical to assume that the evil reputation of the dragon in Europe reflected an ancient struggle between the white race and the yellow race, for a dragon standard was often carried by Oriental warriors. But this theory too is completely unsupportable.

Naturalist Richard Carrington pushes the origin of the dragon further back, to the psychology which lay behind the beginnings of religious thought. Carrington speculates that the dragon originated in an emotion he calls "cosmic fear." Carrington writes: "It is born of [man's] consciousness of his own self, of his wonder at the mystery and immensity of the Universe around him, and above all of the terrifying realization of his own loneliness and insignificance."

More specifically Carrington speculates that the dragon was created in men's minds as a creature of night. For primitive man the night did hold very real terrors. Perhaps each night he wondered if the sun really would return again. Symbolically, then, night could be viewed as a struggle between the good sun god and the evil dragon of darkness. Dawn represented the victory of the sun god over the dragon. The ancient belief in this nightly struggle is represented in the persistent legends of battles between heroes or saints and dragons.

This hypothesis sounds reasonable enough, but we naturally have no way of testing its truth, and we never will. We are on firmer ground when we try to determine why this symbol of overpowering evil took the particular form that it did. What creature inspired the legend of the dragon?

First we must figure out just what a dragon looks like. Actually, even in European lore dragons come in an astonishing variety of shapes and forms. Dragons may have four legs, two legs, or no legs at all. They may or may not have wings. Some have forked tongues or pointed tails or possess a variety of fringes, frills, crests, or other adornments. While dragons are usually scaly, they may also be partially feathered or furred. But all dragons have three features in common—they are large, long, and basically reptilian in appearance. (We must overlook such monsters as the Biblical red dragon of the Apocalypse, which had seven heads and ten horns, and seven crowns upon his heads. The inspiration for such a vision was probably the classical myth of the hydra, and had nothing to do with the ordinary dragon.)

Of all the creatures that have ever existed on the face of the earth those which most closely resemble the dragon are the dinosaurs. Museum reconstructions of dinosaurs quickly conjure up thoughts of dragons. It would not be out of place to envision Saint George battling a stegosaur or the Archangel Michael casting a tyrannosaur out of heaven. But, in fact, dragon and dinosaur almost certainly had nothing to do with one another. The dinosaurs have been dead and gone for some seventy million years.

Dr. Edgard Dacque, formerly a professor of geology at the University of Munich once proposed that the dinosaurs of old were indeed the foundation for the dragon legend. He hauled in the theory of "racial memory" to explain how the enormous time gap was bridged.

But the concept of "racial memory" is, to say the very least, doubtful. Ten thousand years ago our ancestors hunted the mammoth and other elephantlike creatures throughout Europe. Yet European tradition and folklore contains nothing of elephants or elephantlike creatures. The elephants of Asia and Africa were a surprise and a wonder to the Europeans. "Racial memory," it seems, could not bridge the gap of thousands of years, but we are asked to believe that it somehow bridged a gap of millions of years, from a time when there were no men, but only a tiny furry creature that scrambled at the feet of the giant ruling reptiles.

Is there a possibility that some dinosaurs survived into fairly recent times, and that these survivors gave rise to the dragon legend? Evidence for the possible survival of dinosaurs will be discussed in greater detail in a later chapter, but paleontologists most emphatically deny the possibility of dinosaurian survival. It is safe to assume that no dinosaur, dead or alive, was the basis upon which the great dragon legend was built.

Was the inspiration for the dragon legend really some montrous lizard? Charles Gould, who wrote a book called *Mythical Monsters*, thought so. He could even describe the beast. "We may infer that it was a long terrestrial lizard, hibernating, and carnivorous, with the power of constricting with its snake-like body and tail; possibly furnished with winglike expansions of its integument . . . and capable of occasional progress on its hind legs alone, when excited in attack . . . Probably it preferred sandy, open country to forest land . . . Although terrestrial, it probably, in common with most reptiles, enjoyed frequent bathing, and when not so engaged, or basking in the sun, secluded itself under some overhanging bank or cavern."

Most lizards of today are very small, but there is one, the great monitor lizard that lives only on the island of Komodo in the East Indies, which at least roughly answers Gould's profile. The creature looks so much like a dragon that when it was finally discovered by Europeans in 1912 it was called the Komodo dragon. But the range of the Komodo dragon is very restricted, and as far as we know always has been. Nor are there any other large modern lizards which seem to have served as models for the dragon. We must look elsewhere for the origins of the dragon.

If the form of the Western dragon can be laid to any single source, it was man's observations of, and attitude toward another modern reptile—the snake. At first the identification seems unlikely, for the dragon seems to be more like a large lizard than a legless snake. But upon closer examination of some of the dragon lore of the West the creature quickly betrays his serpentine origins.

The word dragon can be traced back to a Greek word meaning sharp-sighted one, an appropriate epithet for the beady-eyed snake. In Latin the Greek word was converted to *draco,* and it meant giant snake. To Pliny the dragon was definitely a giant snake, probably some sort of python. In writing of the dragon of India, which he said was the largest in the world, Pliny observed that it was "so enormous a size as easily to envelop the elephant with its folds and encircle them with its coils. The contest is equally fatal to both; the elephant, vanquished, falls to the earth and by its weight crushes the dragon which is entwined about it."

Pliny added a few more details about dragons. There were dragons in Ethiopia, he said, but these were a mere thirty feet long, and therefore much smaller than the Indian dragons. Actually the longest Old World snake is the reticulated python of India which reaches a length of thirty feet. Pliny had greatly exaggerated the length of the python but length of a large snake is hard to estimate. Although pythons do strangle their prey, no python would ever attack an elephant.

Pliny also noted that African dragons had crests and somewhat dubiously tells of how dragons that live near the African coast go sailing. "Four or five of them twisted and interlaced together . . . setting sail with their heads erect, they are borne along upon the waves to find better sources of nourishment in Arabia."

In the Bible the concept of the dragon and the snake are often interchangeable. The verse from Revelation quoted earlier refers to "the great dragon . . . that old serpent, called the Devil and Satan . . ." Professor H. W. F. Saggs, a specialist in Semetic languages, has suggested that in cuneiform, the ancient written language of Palestine, the word "dragon" really meant "red serpent."

During the seventeenth century, naturalists knew that dragon meant large snake. Konrad Gesner, "the father of zoology," published many books on animals, and at the time of his death was working on his book on snakes. The half-finished manuscript was later edited and published by others. Gesner made it clear that when the ancients talked about dragons they were talking about giant snakes of the python variety. He also pointed out that the old German word for dragon, *Lindwurm,* really meant snake-worm, or even snake-snake. The old Anglo-Saxon word *Wyrm* has been translated as meaning equally dragon, serpent, or worm. Beowulf's dragon is called the Worm, and in old English ballads dragons are called the "laidly [loathly] Worm." Over in Ireland dragonlike monsters were called "direful Wurms."

In an English version of Gesner's work, *Historie of Serpents,* published in 1608, translated and edited by Edward Topsell, Pliny's story of the giant constricting snakes or dragons killing elephants is retold this way:

"They [the dragons] hide themselves in trees, covering their head and letting the other part hang downe like a rope. In those trees they watch untill the Elephant comes to eate and croppe of the branches; then suddenly, before he be aware, they leape into his face and digge out his eyes. Then doe they claspe themselves about his necke, and with their tayles or hinder parts, beate and vexe the Elephant, untill they have made him breathlesse, for they strangle him with theyr fore parts as they beate him with the hinder . . . And this is the disposition of the Dragon, that he never setteth upon the Elephant but with the advantage of the place, and namely from some high tree or rock."

As late as the seventeenth century, men of science revered the classical authors. If Pliny said that dragons attacked elephants, then it must be so. But obviously Topsell had picked up additional information about the habits of the great snakes, as well as a good deal of new misinformation.

The interchangeable nature of serpents and dragons was a feature of folklore as well as natural science. Take for example the English folk tale of the Lambton Worm. Somewhere about 1420, so the story goes, a young nobleman named John Lambton of County Durham went fishing on Sunday, rather than going to church like a good Christian lad should. As a result, instead of a fish the young man pulled from the water "a worm of most unseemly and disgusting appearance." The horrified young man threw the creature into a well (later known as "Worm Well") and tried to forget about it. Naturally, the "worm" and all the disasters that it caused were said to be the result of the young man's ignoring his religious obligations by fishing on Sunday. But this detail is doubtless a later Christian addition to a legend which surely predates 1420, the Lambton family, and Christianity itself.

The worm grew and grew, soon spilling out of the well, and making its home on a nearby hill from which it made regular forays into the farms and homes on the estate of Lord Lambton.

Young John Lambton gave up fishing on Sunday and other sinful activities and embarked to the Holy Land on one of the Crusades. When he returned he found that the worm still held the district in terror. No one could kill it, although many had tried, because the worm had the power to reunite the severed portions of its body. (Folklore attributes this ability to many snakes.) Sir John, with a little magical help, was able to discover a method of killing the monster.

The ending of the story, however, was not entirely happy. Sir John had to swear that after killing the worm he would also kill the next living thing he saw, or his family would be placed under a curse. To get around this restriction a plan was devised. On a signal from Sir John that he had slain the worm a dog would be released. Sir John would kill it and thus avoid the curse. But fate is fate, and plans like this never work in folk tales. The young man's father was so overjoyed on seeing the signal that the worm had been killed that he rushed out of the castle and was the first living thing to meet his son's eyes. Rather than kill his own father Sir John submitted to the curse which held that no Lord of Lambton for nine descending generations would die in bed. The next nine Lords of Lambton obligingly bowed to tradition by dying violently.

When sculptors got around to depicting Sir John in the act of killing the "worm," they showed him sticking a sword into a conventional dragon. There was no contradiction.

The dragon owes its name and basic form to the giant snake—this is too well documented to be disputable. Although the size of the dragon came from the great python, the dragon's reputed ability to breathe fire doubtless came from the smaller poisonous snakes. Gesner, whose description of dragons came from the pythons, correctly noted that "the dragons have little or no venom." But poisonous snakes obviously became mixed in with the dragon legend. To the ancients it must have seemed nearly supernatural that such a small creature as a snake could cause violent death with a single bite.

Generations of retelling the stories of poisonous snakes could easily have resulted in tales of fire-breathing creatures. The progression must have been thus: From the poison injected by the snake's fangs might grow the idea that it was the creature's very breath, not its bite, that was deadly. From poisonous breath it is only a short mental step to fiery breath. Encounters with snakes like the spitting cobra, which do not need to bite their victims to poison them, might have added to the fiery-breath legend.

Topsell talks about the dragon's "vaporous and venemous breath" in discussing how the dragons of Phrygia catch birds. He notes that according to some observers the birds are "drawne by the breath of the dragon as by a thing they love." Topsell himself believed that it was the poisonous breath, "sent up from the dragon to them, that poysoneth and infecteth the ayre about them, whereby their senses are taken from them, and they astonished fall downe into his mouth."

Gould, incidentally, puts a much more pleasant interpretation upon the tale of birds dropping into the dragon's mouth:

"The idea of its fondness for swallows, and power of attracting them, mentioned in some traditions, may not impossibly have been derived from these birds hawking round and through its open jaws in the pursuit of the flies attracted by the viscid humours of its mouth. We know that at the present day a bird, the *trochilus* of the ancients, freely enters the open mouth of the crocodile, and rids it of the parasites affecting its teeth and jaws."

Under their own name snakes have been attributed qualities scarcely less fabulous than those of the dragon. They are supposed to be extremely wise, particularly in healing (note the twisted snake symbol for medicine). They are also supposed to be immortal, or at least very long-lived, and they are supposed to possess great wealth which they guard like misers.

We can only speculate on how the snake picked up this sort of reputation. Perhaps the way in which a snake sheds its skin gave observers thousands of years ago the idea that the creature somehow or other constantly renewed itself with each shedding and thus went on living forever. From here the association of ideas might have been carried a step further: long life usually meant the accumulation of great wisdom, and if the snake were nearly immortal then it surely must know something about health. Long life would also give the snake time to accumulate great wealth. The generally secretive habits of most snakes certainly gives the impression that they are hiding something of value.

Like the dragon, the snake too often has a dual nature. It is extraordinarily powerful, but is this power to be used for good or evil? In Western tradition the snake is almost exclusively evil. In the most ancient piece of literature we have, the Gilgamesh Epic, composed in Mesopotamia sometime in the fourth millenia B.C., or even earlier, the snake is the villain. It is a snake that steals the hard-won plant of immortality from the hero Gilgamesh. The snakes become immortal and mankind is doomed to die. The evil repute in which the people of the ancient Middle East held the serpent is continually reflected throughout the Old Testament.

The ancient Egyptians, on the other hand, used a snake, the deadly cobra, as a symbol of royalty. There exists a charming Egyptian tale concerning a shipwrecked sailor whose life is saved by a magical serpent. Quetzalcoatl, the premier god of the pre-Columbian civilizations of South America, has as his symbol the feathered serpent, which often looks suspiciously dragonlike.

Most of the fabulous qualities of the serpent were later appended to the dragon. In medieval romances dragons were usually extremely ancient and often guarded fabulous treasures. Dragons did not willingly dispense healing knowledge, but bathing in a dragon's blood or eating a dragon's flesh had magical effects. The dragon Fafnir of Teutonic legend (often portrayed in art as a giant snake) had all the qualities of a classic dragon. He guarded a great treasure and he was killed in battle by a hero, Siegfried. When Siegfried bathed in the dragon's blood his skin was hardened and made immune to any weapon. Naturally Siegfried had one vulnerable spot on his back where the leaf of a lime tree prevented the magical blood from reaching his skin. Later he was stabbed to death in this spot. When Siegfried touched the blood of the dragon to his lips, he was immediately able to understand the language of the birds.

Even in Europe, where the dragon had the worst possible reputation, there seems to have been an undercurrent of tradition which pictured the dragon as the good guy—the powerful benefactor of a segment of mankind. The Vikings sailed behind dragon-prowed ships. (In truth the Vikings probably carved images of a number of mythological creatures on the prows of their ships, but these have all been lumped together under the familiar name of dragon.)

In England dragons faired pretty well despite Saint George. Uther, according to legend the father of King Arthur, had the title Pendragon, which can loosely be translated as "head dragon." It was a vision of flaming dragons in the sky which announced to Uther that he would become king. In response Uther made the dragon a royal symbol. Hundreds of years later Richard Coeur-de-Lion carried a dragon standard to the Holy Land in the Crusades. So common was the dragon as a military emblem that some cavalrymen were nicknamed dragons or "dragoons" after their standard. How the tradition of the dragon as a benevolent creature reached Europe is difficult to determine. Perhaps it was just a symbol of power, meant to strike terror into the hearts of enemies. Here was an announcement that "we are as terrible and implacable as dragons, resistance is useless."

Although there is no doubt that the dragon legend began with snakes, there is also no doubt that most dragons since the Middle Ages are depicted as having legs, and look more like lizards. Gesner might have been a great help if he had ever completed his book on snakes and dragons. He discusses how the dragon was really a large constricting snake, and then the text jumps immediately to dragons with feet and wings. The manscript is clearly incomplete.

How the lizard entered the picture, we therefore cannot be sure but we can guess. Lizards throughout the world are for the most part small and harmless creatures, much less impressive than the snakes. The famous Komodo dragon, largest of the living lizards, can grow up to twelve feet in length, not as big as the dragons of legend, but a very big and impressive lizard nonetheless. It may have been heard of in Europe long before it was "discovered." Fanciful and exaggerated accounts of this huge lizard, or other large tropical lizards, probably added to the general belief in dragons.

European dragons are also commonly shown as possessing wings. They are generally short stumpy little things, pathetically small from an aerodynamic point of view and obviously incapable of lifting the monster's huge body off the ground. Although dragons have wings they are rarely depicted as actually flying.

Where did the dragon get its wings? We don't really know but there are several possible explanations. As we have seen before, man tends to piece together parts of different animals when he creates a mythological creature. The dragon may simply have been given the wings of a bat because both dragon and bat had supernaturally evil associations. The wings given to most dragons do have a distinctly batlike appearance.

A far more sensational explanation is that the winged dragon was inspired by "racial memory" of the pterosaurs, the great flying reptiles of the Mesozoic era. Since the pterosaurs were contemporaries of the dinosaurs, the racial memory theory runs into the same objections. The idea that some pterosaurs survived the millions of years from the time of their presumed extinction until the appearance of man on earth can also be discounted for the moment. The pterosaurs, although they are often referred to as "flying dragons," have nothing to do with the winged dragons of legend and folklore. A mere glance at a reconstruction of a pterosaur will show that it looks nothing at all like a dragon. Although the dragon's wings are ludicrously small, those of the pterosaurs are enormous, indeed the creature is practically all wing.

A third explanation is that the winged dragon of legend began when Europeans saw or heard of a tiny lizard from the Malay Archipelago, *Draco volans* or the "flying dragon." This flying or, more properly, gliding lizard has enormously elongated ribs. These rib extensions are connected by a leathery membrane and can be unfolded. The membrane then becomes stretched between them to form "wings" with which the creature can glide up to fifteen feet, from tree to tree. But *Draco volans* is only a few inches long, hardly the sort of beast to inspire terror and monster legends. Yet it is possible that exaggerated tales of the little lizard reached Europe and helped to start the flying dragon legend. Even more likely is that dried specimens of *Draco volans* were brought to Europe and sold as "baby dragons." In either case, however, the idea of the flying dragon seems already to have existed, and *Draco volans* was only confirmation.

Perhaps the most persuasive support for the idea of the flying dragon was supplied by simple trickery. We have already discussed Jenny Hanivers, basilisks, sea monks, and other manufactured natural wonders. It is hardly possible that the forgers who constructed these curiosities could avoid the temptations of manufacturing and selling dragons. Of course manufactured dragons were, of necessity, small and had to be passed off as "baby dragons."

Preserved "baby dragons" it seems were fairly common in collections of curiosities. The Italian mathematician and physician Hieronimus Cardanus saw five dried "baby dragons" in Paris in 1557. He described them thus: "Two footed creatures with wings so small that, in my opinion, they could hardly fly with them. Their heads were small and shaped like the heads of snakes, they were of pleasant color without feathers or hair and the largest of them was as large as a wren."

At about the time Cardanus saw the dried "baby dragons" a Frenchman named Pierre Belon (when writing he Latinized his name to Petrus Bellonius) printed a picture of a winged dragon, which became the standard for all later pictures. It looked very much like the two-footed and winged creature described by Cardanus. In 1640 a book called *The History of Serpents and Dragons* by Ulisse Aldrovandi was published containing a drawing of a two-footed winged dragon that was basically a more elegant rendering of Pierre Belon's drawing. The Aldrovandi dragon has been reprinted countless times and has become the standard for all later dragon pictures.

Since our popular conception of the dragon seems to depend so heavily on those five dried "baby dragons" that were displayed in Paris in 1557, we might speculate for a moment as to what they were. The most logical explanation seems to be that they were manufactured objects—small lizards with bat wings or parts of bat wings grafted on to the side and one pair of legs amputated. Cardanus was well aware of the possibility of trickery, but stated firmly that the specimens were not manufactured. If they had been, he believed, "they would have received larger wings to be under less suspicion."

Other commentators have taken Cardanus' description and Belon's picture and concluded that these dried specimens were without doubt *Draco volans*, which had been deprived of one of its pairs of legs. However, a comparison of Belon's and Aldrovandi's dragon with photographs of *Draco volans* leaves considerable doubt in this author's mind that the former was inspired by the latter.

In Aldrovandi's book of serpents and dragons there appears the drawing of a particularly fearsome and unusual-looking winged dragon. The creature was described thus: "Its head is serrated, and its crest comes to a peak . . . It has a flexible tail, two feet in length, and bristling with prickles. The skin is like that of a skate." It certainly should have been, for this creature was undoubtedly a skate or ray cut and shaped to the image of a monster. This was a typical Jenny Haniver dragon.

Although preserved specimens of adult dragons never found their way into museums or private collections, the bones of such dragons were commonly displayed. For centuries men had been unearthing gigantic bones of unexplained origin. These were attributed to humanoid giants, unicorns, behemoth and leviathan of the Bible, and a host of other fabulous creatures, including naturally the dragon.

Here at last, you might think, is where the dinosaurs come in. The finding of the bones of dinosaurs inspired dragon legends. But alas, even at this point, dragons and dinosaurs do not meet. Dinosaurs have just been dead for too long. What fossils remain were deeply buried and hard to get at. Although dinosaur fossils had undoubtedly been found many times throughout history, the whole concept of giant reptiles was only developed during the nineteenth century. When naturalists and collectors re-examined their collections in the light of the new knowledge of dinosaurs and other giant reptiles, they found they had relatively few fossils of this type. What they did possess in great abundance were the bones of more recently extinct giants—giant mammals.

Today the world contains a relatively small number of really large animals. But some ten thousand years ago great herds of mammoths roamed Europe and North America. Rhinoceroses of various sorts and bears as big as the biggest known today were common throughout the Northern Hemisphere.

The study of paleontology and comparative anatomy are quite new. Learned men of three centuries ago could look at the skull of an extinct elephant and say that it was the remains of a gigantic cyclops, like Polyphemus of Homer's *Odyssey*. The enlarged nasal passage in an elephant's skull does look rather like an enormous single eye socket. But no amount of anatomical ignorance could convert the skull of a rhinoceros or bear into that of a human giant. Such skulls had to become something else, and they usually became dragons.

How dragon legends were spun from the bones of extinct mammals has been beautifully illustrated by the late Willy Ley.

In the market place in the city of Klagenfurt in Austria, says Ley, is a rather impressive monument. "The monument, fashioned about the year 1590, shows a naked giant in the act of slaying a dragon with a big spiked club. The dragon has a body similar to that of a crocodile, with bat wings attached, and is furiously spitting at the giant—fire in the legend, water in the monument. It is the skull of this dragon that is interesting. Aside from its somewhat incongruous leaf ears, it displays very clearly the outlines of the skull of woolly *Rhinoceros antiquitatis,* one of the contemporaries of the woolly mammoth. Chroniclers state that the skull of the 'dragon' was found near Klagenfurt about the middle of the sixteenth century, three decades before the monument was erected. The skull itself was kept in the Town Hall. It has been repeatedly examined by modern scientists and found to be the skull of the woolly rhinoceros."

The traditional home of the European dragon is a cave, and the mountains of Central Europe are dotted with reputed "dragon caves" and "dragon grottos." In 1673 a German physician, Pattersonius Hayn, explored some of these caves in the Little Carpathians in Hungary. He found several strange skulls which he identified as belonging to dragons. On the strength of his finds Hayn wrote a learned paper on "Dragon Skulls in the Carpathians."

Similar finds in the caves of Transylvania inspired a German naturalist named Vollgand to write an article on "Transylvanian Dragons." Vollgand's paper was illustrated with drawings of the skulls and reconstructions of the creature to which they were supposed to have belonged. The drawings show clearly that the bones were those of cave bears, while the reconstructions pictured the typical winged dragon.

The erudite Jesuit Father Athanasius Kircher was one of the more daring thinkers of the seventeenth century. Well educated, but also uncritically enthusiastic, Father Kircher's wild speculations often made him the object of ridicule. He wrote on every aspect of science from archaeology to zoology. In *Ecstatic Voyage* he described conditions on other planets according to the astrological concepts of the time. In his book on zoology he tried to list all the animals that had not perished in the Flood. He even went so far as to picture the types of cages Noah had used for the different kinds of animals.

Father Kircher's main contribution to dragon lore was made in his book on volcanoes, *The Subterranean World.* He attributed the existence of volcanoes to a vast number of subterranean caves. Most of these caves were filled with water or fire, but a few contained only air. In these air-filled caves lived the dragons of the world. Being underground creatures who rarely ventured to the surface, they were quite naturally not seen very often. Those few individuals who were encountered on the surface were unfortunate wanderers who had somehow blundered into the sunlit world, and were then prevented from returning to their underground homes because an earthquake or some other natural catastrophe had blocked the way back.

An incidental example of Father Kircher's enthusiasm can be seen in his reaction to Belon's drawing of a dragon. Kircher unhesitatingly stated the dragon in the picture was the notorious "Dragon of Rhodes" slain in 1345 by Deodatus of Gozon, a brave knight. The bones of this dragon were supposed to have been found in a cave near the site of the battle.

So there, in more or less of a nutshell, we have the history of the Western dragon. The myth started perhaps with a generalized fear of creatures of the darkness. The dragon got its name and many of its characteristics from the giant constricting snakes, as described by Greek and Roman authors. The terror of small poisonous snakes later contributed to the dragon the ability to breathe fire. The addition of wings and legs came later still. These may have been added by stories of large lizards or crocodiles and of the tiny "winged" lizard *Draco volans*. The bones of giant mammals, found so often in the caves of Europe, completed the case for the existence of the dragon.

The origins of the Oriental dragon myth are quite different and even more obscure than those of the Western dragon myth. The Oriental dragon is even more heavily and obviously mythological than its Western counterpart. There were no Chinese Plinys or Gesners to classify different kinds of dragons.

The two forms of dragons, however, have a few things in common in addition to their generally reptilian appearance. They are both powerful and reputed to be the guardians of great fortunes. (In both East and West the figure of a dragon is commonly displayed at entrances and on doors. From its treasure-guarding activities the dragon has come to be thought of as a guardian.) Although Western dragons were known as evil misers, one rarely encountered an Oriental dragon without coming away with a generous gift.

Oriental dragons could occasionally be capricious and even malevolent, but they were usually benevolent. Western dragons were solitary while Oriental dragons lived in Chinese-style societies. There was, for example, a hierarchy of dragon bureaucrats.

Although it often looks more snakelike than the Western dragon the Oriental dragon is not a glorified serpent. The snake has no better a reputation in the East than it does in the West. In China the snake along with the scorpion, centipede, frog, and lizard is classified as one of the five poisonous creatures who must be placated at regular festivals.

In a cave in the mountains near Hangchow, so the legend goes, lived the White Snake, an immortal, exceedingly powerful and exceedingly evil serpent who was responsible for numerous disasters. The snake's plan to destroy the city of Hangchow was foiled only through the intervention of a Buddhist priest who imprisoned the creature in a box and buried it beneath the Pagoda of Thunder and Wind. Some of the people of the province believed that the White Snake was responsible for the Japanese invasion of Manchuria in 1931. Shortly before the invasion the Pagoda of Thunder and Wind was destroyed during a storm.

Dragons from different parts of the Orient looked different. The Chinese dragon or Lung has been described as an animal with "a camel's head, a deer's horns, a rabbit's eyes, a cow's ears, a snake's neck, a frog's belly, a carp's scales, a hawk's claws, and a tiger's palms." It is hard to imagine what such a conglomerate would look like. Fortunately, the usual representations of the Chinese dragon do not fit this description.

The number of claws the dragon possesses seems to have some significance. The Imperial dragon of the Manchus had five claws on each foot. The ordinary Chinese dragon had four, whereas the dragon most commonly represented in Japan had a mere three toes.

Carrington suggests that both East and West were subject to the same sort of myth building concerning the powers of light or good and darkness or evil. He writes: "There was, however, so far as the dragon was concerned an extremely important difference. Instead of finding itself allied with the powers of darkness, and therefore appearing as the villain of the piece it seems to have been cast in exactly the opposite role. The part of the sun god of Western mythology is assumed in the East by the dragon, and the more sinister natural forces are largely identified with other symbolical beings such as demons and snakes."

As with the Western dragon, many once believed (and some still do) that the stories began with a real, but unknown giant reptile. Dr. N. B. Dennys, a nineteenth-century expert on Chinese mythology, held that there was "little doubt" that there once had been real dragons in China.

Thrilling as Dr. Dennys' suggestion was, there is "little doubt" that there never was a real dragon in China. The form of the mythical dragons were probably taken from a much more ordinary creature, but if it was not a snake what was it? One of the qualities of the mythical dragon offers a clue. Oriental dragons were intimately associated with all aspects of life and the natural world, but they had particularly strong associations with water. Dragons lived in lakes and rivers and seas and even in raindrops. Dragons controlled the tides and waves, created or stopped floods, and were the guardians of the rainfall. So for the ancestor of the dragon we must look to a water animal.

The best candidate for the ancestor of the Oriental dragon is the Chinese alligator *Alligator sinensis*. Today this creature lives only in the lower Yangtze, and is rare. But in historical times it was widespread throughout eastern China. Although not quite as large as the American alligator, it is sufficiently large and powerful to inspire legends. Of course, as with the snake in the West, the Chinese alligator was only a starting point. Around it crystallized a host of often unrelated legends. Even its form changed dramatically as it acquired a camel's head, deer's horns, and the rest. When Europeans first learned of this creature, they translated all the names under which it was known as one word—dragon.

Like the Europeans, the Chinese also mistook the bones of ancient and extinct mammals for those of departed dragons. While the bones of the evil Western dragons were regarded as mere curiosities, the bones of the benevolent Oriental dragon were reputed to have great healing powers. The Chinese pharmacopoeia, accumulated over the long centuries of Chinese civilization, is a marvelously long and detailed collection of remedies. Virtually every known substance, if properly prepared, was thought to be a cure for some sort of disease. But of all the cures dragon bones were the most effective. There were three types of dragon bones, *Lung-Koo,* ordinary dragon bones; *Fun-Lung-Chee,* large white dragon teeth; and *Tsing-Lung-Chee,* small black dragon teeth.

These dragon bones and teeth were usually discovered by accident when a fossil deposit was exposed by erosion or landslide. Since fossil bones are sometimes washed out of hillsides by strong rains the sudden appearance of such fossils after a rainstorm might have helped to strengthen the association of dragons and water.

These "dragon bones" and teeth were dug up and sent to drugstores in Peking, Hong Kong, and other metropolitan areas of China. There they were ground up and sold, often at very high prices, as medicine. Europeans, by the way, have no right to snicker at the medical theories of the "superstitious" Chinese. In Europe some fossils were labeled "unicorn horns," and since the unicorn was a magical and beneficent creature, like the Chinese dragon, such "unicorn horns" were ground up and sold as cures, just as the dragon bones were. So popular was the unicorn remedy that the unicorn still appears in the crest of the apothecaries' guild.

During the nineteenth century, however, the Europeans had lost interest in downing powdered "unicorn horns" and had recognized the Chinese "dragon bones" for the fossils they were. Western travelers in China who had paleontological interests or training never failed to do some browsing in the local drugstore in the hope that the dragon bone cabinets would contain some rare and valuable fossils. Most of the fossils were common and of fairly recent origin. But occasionally they found a treasure.

It was clues found among the Chinese druggist's "dragon bones" that led paleontologists to the caves at Chou-Kou Tien. There they discovered the remains of a creature far more remarkable than any dragon. The caves contained the bones of Peking man, one of our own ancestors.

This seems a rather fitting note upon which to end our excursion into the land of the dragons. The secret of the dragon caves, as it turns out, was really our own primitive selves.

The Great Sea Serpent

The frigate H.M.S. *Daedalus* put into Plymouth Harbor on October 4, 1848. Within a few hours of the time it docked, the strangest rumors were circulating throughout the town. It was said that the captain and some of the officers and crew had seen a gigantic sea serpent while sailing between the Cape of Good Hope and St. Helena Island. Wild-sounding stories concerning the *Daedalus* sea serpent appeared in the press. Since the sea serpent had become associated with error and fraud, the stories tended to reflect discredit on the Royal Navy. The Admiralty quickly stepped in and asked Captain Peter M'Quhae of the *Daedalus* either to deny the sea serpent report or openly state just exactly what he and his men had seen.

Almost by return mail Admiral Sir W. H. Gage received Captain M'Quhae's reply. If the Admiralty had been expecting a denial, the captain's letter must have come as quite a shock:

"Sir, In reply to your letter of this day's date [Oct. 11], information as to the truth of a statement published in *The Times* newspaper, of a sea-serpent of extraordinary dimensions having been seen from Her Majesty's ship *Daedalus*, under my command, on her passage from the East Indies, I have the honour to acquaint you, for the information of my Lords Commissioners of the Admiralty, that at 5 o'clock P. M. on the 6th of August last, in latitude 24°44's, and longitude 9°22'E., the weather dark and cloudy, wind fresh from the N.W., with a long ocean swell from the S.W., the ship on the port tack heading N.E. by N., something very unusual was seen by Mr. Sartoris, midshipman, rapidly approaching the ship from before the beam. The circumstance was immediately reported by him to the officer of the watch, Lieut. Edgar Drummond, with whom and Mr. William Barrett, the Master, I was at the time walking the quarter-deck. The ship's company were at supper.

"On our attention being called to the object it was discovered to be an enormous serpent, with head and shoulders kept about four feet constantly above the surface of the sea, and as nearly as we could approximate by comparing it with the length of what our main topsail yard would show in the water, there was at the very least 60 feet of the animal a *fleur d'eau,* no portion of which was, to our perception, used in propelling it through the water, either by vertical or horizontal undulation. It passed rapidly, but so close under our lee quarter, that had it been a man of my acquaintance, I should easily have recognised his features with the naked eye; and it did not, either in approaching the ship or after it had passed our wake deviate in the slightest degree from its course to the S.W., which it held on at the pace of from 12 to 15 miles per hour, apparently on some determined purpose.

"The diameter of the serpent was about 15 or 16 inches

behind the head, which was, without any doubt, that of a snake, and it was never during the 20 minutes that it continued in the sight of our glasses, once below the surface of the water; its colour a dark brown, with yellowish white about the throat. It had no fins, but something like a mane of a horse, or rather a bunch of seaweed, washed about its back. It was seen by the quartermaster, the boatswain's mate, and the man at the wheel, in addition to myself and the officers above mentioned.

"I am having a drawing of the serpent made from a sketch taken immediately after it was seen, which I hope to have ready for transmission to my Lords Commissioners of the Admiralty by to-morrow's post. I have, etc. Peter M'Quhae, Captain."

Several excellent drawings made from Captain M'Quhae's sketch were shortly published by the *Illustrated London News,* and have become the most celebrated of all sea serpent drawings.

Captain M'Quhae's written account was publicly supported by two other officers of the *Daedalus.* Lieutenant Edgar Drummond allowed the notes he had made after the encounter to be published. The significant portions are quoted below:

"We observed a most remarkable fish on our lee quarter, crossing the stern in a S.W. direction; the appearance of its head which, with the back fin, was the only portion of the animal visible, was long pointed and flattened at the top, perhaps ten feet in length, the upper jaw projecting considerably: the fin was perhaps twenty feet in the rear of the head, and visible occasionally; the captain also asserted that he saw the tail, or another fin about the same distance behind it; the upper part of the head and shoulders appeared of a dark brown colour, and beneath the under jaw a brownish white.

"It pursued a steady undeviating course, keeping its head horizontal with the surface of the water and in rather a raised position, disappearing occasionally beneath a wave for a very brief interval, and not apparently for purposes of respiration. It was going at the rate of perhaps from twelve to fourteen miles an hour, and when nearest was perhaps one hundred yards distant: in fact it gave one quite the idea of a large snake or eel."

A letter to the *Times* from a seaman who had once mistaken a piece of giant seaweed for a sea serpent and assumed the men of the *Daedalus* had done the same inspired the third public defense of the sea serpent, by a man who had seen it. An unnamed "Officer of Her Majesty's Ship *Daedalus*" wrote a strong response to the seaweed theory:

"I beg to state that the object seen from Her Majesty's ship on that occasion was beyond all question, a living animal, moving rapidly through the water against a cross sea, and within five points of a fresh breeze, with such velocity that the water was surging under its chest as it passed along at a rate probably, of not less than 10 miles per hour.

"Captain M'Quhae's first impulse was to tack in pursuit, ourselves being on wind on the larboard tack, when he reflected that we neither could lay up for it nor overhaul it in speed. There was nothing to be done, therefore, but to observe it as accurately as we could with our glasses as it came up under our lee quarter and passed away to windward, at its nearest position being not more than 200 yards from us, the eye, the mouth, the nostril, the colour and form all being most distinctly visible to us.

"We all felt greatly astonished at what we saw, though there were sailors among us of 30 and 40 years standing, who had traveled most seas and seen many marvels in their day. The captain was the first to exclaim: 'This must be that animal called the sea-serpent' a conclusion we all at last settled down to. My impression was that it was rather of a lizard than a serpentine character, as its movement was steady and uniform, as if propelled by fins, not by an undulatory power."

Ever since man has been going down to the sea in ships, sailors have returned with tales of the enormous and strange creatures they have seen plying the waves. Sometimes these tales described creatures that were later caught, classified, named, and mounted in a museum. All those creatures that did not seem to fit into the known classifications became lumped under the title the Great Sea Serpent, a misnomer since many of the creatures described were quite unserpent-like in appearance. But the name sea serpent has been around for so long that we are stuck with it, accurate or not.

Of all the sea serpent stories that of the *Daedalus* is very probably the best on record.

Usually sea serpents have been reported by men whose reliability was doubtful. There have been a large number of sea serpent hoaxes. For example, stories would appear in the press about how a particular ship had sighted a sea serpent when in truth no such ship ever existed. Such stories are surprisingly difficult to check out, particularly if they are many years old. In other cases the sighting might have been made by a single individual, or made under conditions which made careful observation virtually impossible. Some sightings were not written down until months or years after the event had taken place, allowing time to blur and alter the facts of the original encounter.

None of these pitfalls occur in the case of the *Daedalus* sea serpent. There is no doubt that there was a ship *Daedalus* and that a number of the men on it reported seeing a strange sea creature. If the officers had decided to cook up a hoax between them, it was a very dangerous sort of hoax, for it meant not only lying to the public but lying to the Lords of the Admiralty as well, a very, very serious offense. If the hoax had been discovered, the career of Captain M'Quhae and all others who had participated in the hoax with him might have been ruined. If the men of the *Daedalus* had felt the sighting to be vague or doubtful, they probably would have preferred to remain silent. Although the case received the widest possible publicity, no one has ever successfully impugned the honesty, reliability, and good sense of the men of the *Daedalus*.

Although the weather was described as "dark and squally," the witnesses aboard the *Daedalus* got a good look at the passing monster. Lieutenant Drummond noted, "It was visible to the naked eye for five minutes, and with a glass for perhaps fifteen more."

Captain M'Quhae's boast that had a man of his acquaintance passed as close to the ship as the monster had, "I should easily have recognised his features with the naked eye," cannot be taken lightly.

Following the *Daedalus* report a number of ingenious explanations for the sighting were postulated. None of these was very satisfactory and, as long as the good faith and good sight of the men of the *Daedalus* were accepted, the case remained very much an unexplained mystery—more than a mystery as far as the monster buffs are concerned, for they look upon the *Daedalus* sighting as almost conclusive proof of the existence of the sea serpent. The *Daedalus* sighting started a renewal in interest in the sea serpent which continued into the twentieth century.

While the skeptics have trouble attempting to explain away the *Daedalus* sea serpent as an ordinary creature, the monster buffs who say that the men of the *Daedalus* saw a large unknown sea creature have never faced up adequately to the creature's rather wooden appearance and strange motion. All three published eyewitness reports make mention of these peculiar characteristics.

Captain M'Quhae wrote: "No portion of [the sea serpent] was, to our perception, used in propelling it through the water, either by vertical or horizontal undulation." He also spoke of the monster's "pace of from 12 to 15 miles per hour, apparently on some determined purpose." In Lieutenant Drummond's notes appear the words, "It pursued a steady, undeviating course, keeping its head horizontal with the surface of the water." The unnamed officer who wrote to the *Times* guessed that its form was that of a lizard, rather than a snake, because "its movement was steady and uniform, as if propelled by fins, not by any undulatory power."

Over the years monster buffs have expanded on this idea of underwater fins, by proposing that the *Daedalus* monster was anything from a plesiosaur, a long-necked and finned marine reptile from the age of dinosaurs, to some sort of unknown but gigantic seal with a long neck. But no one aboard the *Daedalus* observed any wash created by the motion of fins or flippers, and, besides, the propulsion of the creature is only part of the puzzle. The above-water portion of the monster seems to have been curiously motionless. Although it passed close by the ship none of the witnesses mention its turning its head to get a better look. The *Daedalus* must certainly have been as unsual looking to the monster as the monster was to the *Daedalus*. Even the picture of the monster is bothersome, for it is shown as having a back straight as a board. The *Daedalus* sea serpent does not look like a living creature. What then could it be?

Just a few years ago L. Sprague de Camp, a writer of science fact and fantasy, and a man with a powerful interest in those fringe areas where fact and fancy are sometimes indistinguishable, took another look at one of the drawings of the *Daedalus* sea serpent. He squinted his eyes and was suddenly struck by an inspiration.

"If one looks at the *Illustrated London News* picture

squint-eyed," he wrote, "one sees that the 'serpent' looks like a dugout canoe, of the kind used in primitive lands for fishing. The dark color of the 'serpent's' back would be the shadowed interior of the canoe, and the 'head' the expanded bow platform on which a fisherman places his foot in shooting or spearing a fish."

He theorized that a couple of fishermen from the west coast of Africa or from the coast of Brazil accidently stuck a harpoon into a huge but known sea creature like the whale shark. Whale sharks are reasonably common in tropical waters. Finding themselves attached to a gigantic creature that was quickly pulling them out to sea, the fishermen panicked and jumped overboard.

"This particular shark," continued de Camp, "not seriously hurt but quite indignant took off, towing the canoe like a chip behind it." The whale shark could have towed the canoe around for weeks or even months until the harpoon line broke or rotted away."

"This theory accounts for the curious mode of progress of the serpent in a straight line without visible wriggling. The 'mane' could be either seaweed that had grown on the derelict or water splashing around inside the boat as it labored through the swells or both. Do I hear any objections?"

You bet there were objections. What about the "eye, the mouth, the nostril" reported by one of the witnesses? Canoes do not have faces. But some do have figureheads, or at least painted designs of one sort or another on the prow. Could the canoe have been decorated with the head of a monster, thus helping to confuse the men of the *Daedalus?*

Even more basic is the objection that experienced and responsible seamen could not have mistaken an abandoned canoe for a living creature, no matter how bizarrely the canoe was painted. But perhaps the buffs are wrong to place so much faith in man's powers of observation, particularly at sea. Experienced seamen have often made errors which would seem impossible for any sane and sighted person to make. Nothing proves this more abundantly than the history of the sea serpent. So perhaps the century-old mystery of the *Daedalus* sea serpent may ultimately be solved by studying the fishing habits of the peoples of the South Atlantic littoral, rather than by postulating any sort of large and unknown sea creature. That is the problem with the Great Sea Serpent—it could always have been something else.

Back in 1848 people were as skeptical about the sea serpent as they are today. But it still was a matter of lively controversy, serious enough to be thrashed out in the letter columns of the *Times,* along with all the other important questions of the day. Each well-publicized sighting would stimulate leading scientists to come forth with a theory as to the nature of the beast that had been observed. Never mind that they mostly attempted to explain away the sightings as something known and ordinary, at least they were interested enough to enter the fray.

Over the last few decades the sea serpent has fallen upon bad days. It is not that people have stopped seeing sea serpents. Bernard Heuvelmans, who undoubtedly knows more about sea serpents than anyone else in the world, lists seventy-five reported sightings between the years 1940 and 1966. In better days, between 1900 and 1926 the total number of sightings recorded by Heuvelmans is one hundred and seven, only thirty-two more during the same number of years. This difference might easily be accountable not to a decline in sea serpent appearances but to a decline in interest. People no longer report large and strange creatures. Today, if a person sees what once might unhesitatingly have been called a sea serpent, he assumes that he is making some error in observation, or he simply keeps his mouth shut for fear of ridicule.

Even the newspapers, which could be counted upon to produce at least a paragraph on every sea serpent sighting, no matter how poor a sighting it was, have practically abandoned the beast. Most scientists don't even bother to denounce sea serpents anymore.

As a result of this massive disbelief the monster seems to have lost its self-confidence, becoming shy and retiring. It was not like that in the good old days. A standard part of any ancient sea serpent legend was that the monster was large enough to smash up ships, and hungry and ferocious enough to gobble up hapless sailors right off the deck. But while the ship-smashing sea serpent is at least a possibility in the days of wooden sailing ships it holds few terrors in these days of steel ships. Several accounts even speak of sea serpents being killed after a collision with a modern ship. In addition, today's noisy engine-driven ships might easily frighten off the sea serpents if they were sensitive to sounds as most large sea creatures seem to be. The noise and size of modern ships may also account for the smaller number of sea serpent sightings in modern times. The poor thing is simply being scared off.

From antiquity to the advent of the ironclad, the sea serpent was a creature to be regarded with some terror. The first clear reference we have to sea serpents comes from Aristotle, who wrote in the fourth century B.C.: "In Libya the serpents are very large. Mariners sailing along that coast have told how they have seen the bones of many oxen which, it was apparent to them, had been devoured by the serpents. And as their ships sailed on, the serpents came to attack them, some of them throwing themselves on a trireme and capsizing it." Other classical writers also mentioned great aquatic serpents.

These early tales were undoubtedly inspired by the giant snakes of Africa and Asia, whose appearance had already been impressive enough to begin the legend of the dragon.

The giant snakes are, of course, not aquatic although large pythons have been known to take to the water and swim well. Stories of genuine water snakes and other large and unpleasant snakelike creatures like the conger eel could easily have gotten mixed into the classical descriptions. We have to remember that the classical naturalists based much of their writing on hearsay. It was the best information they could get, but it was hearsay nonetheless.

We can trace the concept of the classical sea serpent through the medieval churchmen and naturalists upon whose works the modern idea of the sea serpent is based. But first there is a curious and puzzling side branch to the story which we must examine—that is the Biblical leviathan, a creature often identified with the Great Sea Serpent.

Even the name leviathan is troublesome because no one knows exactly what it means. It has been translated many ways, most commonly as "tortuous monster," a phrase that certainly makes leviathan sound as though it means large snake. Yet the most complete description of leviathan, that given in Chapter 41 of the Book of Job, gives quite an unsnakelike picture.

"Canst thou draw out leviathan with an hook? . . . I will not conceal his parts, nor his power, nor his comely proportion. . . . Who can open the doors of his face? his teeth are terrible round about. His scales are his pride, shut up together as with a close seal. One is so near to another, that no air can come between them. They are joined one to another, they stick together, that they cannot be sundered. By his neesings a light doth shine, and his eyes are like the eyelids of the morning. . . . In his neck remaineth strength, and sorrow is turned to joy before him. The flakes of his flesh are joined together: they are firm in themselves; they cannot be moved. . . . When he raiseth up himself, the mighty are afraid: . . ."

The description gives many more details of leviathan's power, such as his ability to breathe fire, deflect spear thrusts, and perform other obviously miraculous feats.

The animal which served as inspiration for leviathan is by no means obvious from this description. Some of the statements like "the flakes of his flesh are joined together," which has been taken to mean that leviathan was a creature with webbed feet, and the reference to close-fitting scales and a mouth filled with teeth have led some commentators to the conclusion that leviathan was inspired by a large crocodile. The ancient Hebrews would have been well acquainted with crocodiles.

If leviathan were mentioned only in Job, then the crocodile identification would work. But in Psalm 104, verse 25, there is another and even more famous mention of the mysterious leviathan. "So is this great and wide sea, wherein are things creeping innumerable, both small and great beasts. There go the ships: there is that leviathan, whom thou hast made to play therein."

Here the reference is clearly to a creature of the deep sea, and yet the crocodile, at least any crocodile the ancient Hebrews were likely to have known, was a dweller in rivers and lakes. The statement in Psalms has led to a general assumption that leviathan is a giant whale. But how much contact could the ancient Hebrews have had with giant whales? Forget the story of Jonah and the whale—the reference there is to a big fish of unknown variety. Later translators seem to have injected the idea that the creature that swallowed Jonah was a whale. Besides whales just do not fit with the description given in Job. Whales do not have scales, nor do they have necks.

Two possible solutions to the leviathan puzzle present themselves. Either the leviathan of Job is a crocodile and the leviathan of the Psalms is something else, perhaps a whale, or leviathan really is some sort of genuinely unknown giant sea creature. But we can go no further than this, because there is no more evidence. Leviathan must remain a creature of murky mystery.

The mainstream of sea serpent history picks up once again in the sixteenth century. The principal and perhaps only authority for the sea serpents of that era is the Swede, Olaus Magnus, who was named Roman Catholic Archbishop of Uppsala following the death of his brother, Archbishop Johannes. Since Olaus was living in exile in Italy during the Reformation and had few clerical duties to perform, he set about compiling a very complete history of his northern homeland. In 1539 he had published a map of the northern lands. Olaus dotted the sea around Scandinavia with drawings of huge and terrifying creatures, including a gigantic sea snake which is shown encoiling a sailing ship and gobbling up some sailors. But the map is not entirely the invention of Olaus' imagination, for many of the monsters on it can be recognized as exaggerated versions of real sea creatures, whales, walruses, and the like.

In his book Olaus describes his sea serpent as being two hundred feet long and twenty feet thick. Not only that: "He hath commonly hair hanging from his neck a Cubit long, and sharp Scales, and is black, and he hath flaming shining eyes. This snake disquiets the Shippers, and he puts his head on high like a pillar, and catcheth away men, and he devours them." You can be sure that such a monster would "disquiet" the shippers.

The Archbishop also added: "This [the appearance of a sea serpent] hapneth not, but it signifies some wonderful change of Kingdom near at hand; namely that the Princes shall die, or be banished, or some Tumultuous Wars shall presently follow."

Olaus' last statement has often been quoted by modern

skeptics as proof that Olaus' sea serpent (or Sjö-orm) was nothing more than a magical monster concocted out of the superstitious babblings of a backward people. This judgment, however, is hardly a fair one. To a sixteenth-century church-man all things natural were part of God's plan. Nothing happened by accident, and the sudden appearance of so large and terrifying a creature must have some great significance. Eclipses were also related to great changes in the affairs of men, but this does not mean that eclipses do not really take place.

For two centuries the great encyclopaedists repeated Olaus Magnus' description almost verbatim. They had his sea ser-pent's picture redrawn and included in their own works. But they added little, if anything, that was new and sometimes they expressed reservation about the reality of the sea ser-pent they were describing.

Olaus Magnus must have compiled his description of the sea serpent from traditional sailors' tales and other half-legendary material, but his sources are by no means clear, and we don't know how much of the information came right off the top of his own head. Not until 1734 do we get our first good eyewitness account of the sea serpent. But the account is a classic, for the witness could hardly be more trustworthy. He was Hans Egede, a Norwegian Protestant missionary to Greenland. Pastor Egede's pious and hard-working life earned him the title of Apostle of Greenland. While sailing near the Danish colony of Good Hope on the Davis Strait, Greenland, Egede saw, not a sea serpent, but a sea monster.

"This monster was of so huge a size," he wrote, "that com-ing out of the Water, its Head reached as high as the Mast-Head; its Body was bulky as the Ship and three or four times as long. [Unfortunately we do not know the dimensions of Egede's ship, and cannot accurately calculate the size of his monster. The best estimate is that Egede thought the creature was around a hundred feet long.] It had a long pointed Snout and spouted like a Whale-Fish; great broad Paws, and the Body seemed covered with shell-work, its skin very rugged and uneven. The under part of its Body was shaped like an enormous huge Serpent, and when it dived again under Water, it plunged backwards into the Sea, and so raised its Tail aloft, which seemed a whole ship's length distant from the bulkiest part of its Body." Then unfortunately he added, "That evening we had very bad weather." This comment has led many to class Egede's monster with Olaus' sea serpents.

A map of Egede's voyage drawn by another missionary, Pastor Bing, contained a sketch of the monster, and accompanied Egede's account of his travels. The account of the monster itself is straightforward, almost dry—no mention of the monster devouring sailors or anything like that. The description contains some ambiguous phrases, but this is hardly surprising for Egede was not a writer or a scientist. Pastor Bing's drawing complements the written account well enough, although it shows the monster's head and tail sticking out of the water in a most improbable manner. This picture led a man named Henry Lee, who wrote a book called *Sea Monsters Unmasked,* to conclude that what Egede really saw was a giant squid, with its tail sticking out of the water. According to Lee's interpretation Egede had mistaken the tail of the squid for the head of the monster, and one of the squid's tentacles for the monster's tail. Egede's mention of a body covered with "shell-work" seems to support the squid hypothesis. The major problem with the squid theory is that no one knows if a squid would or could stick its tail high out of the water in the necessary manner.

Perhaps it is unwise to place too much confidence in the accuracy of Pastor Bing's drawing. We do not know whether Bing saw the monster himself, or whether he drew the sketch under Egede's direction, or merely from the written description. Bing was reported to have told his brother-in-law that the monster had red and firey eyes, indicating that he too had seen the creature, but we cannot be sure. It seems quite impossible for any creature, known or unknown, to stick both its head and tail out of the water in the manner of the creature in the drawing. Therefore it is most likely that the artist combined two different parts of the sighting, the first in which the creature's head was high above the water, and later when it dived, and raised its tail.

When Hans Egede wrote his journal he noted the astonishing encounter with the monster without any undue emphasis. He also mentioned seeing several different kinds of whales which he described with great accuracy, indicating that he was both knowledgeable and keen-sighted. However, by the time Egede's son got around to printing his father's journal the monster had grown in importance and a copy of Pastor Bing's drawing was made the frontispiece of the book.

The sea serpent was occupying an ever larger place in the lore of the seafaring Scandinavians. In the middle of the eighteenth century when Erik Pontoppidan, Bishop of Bergen, compiled *A Natural History of Norway* (published in 1752 and 1753), he included a chapter on the wondrous creatures of the northern seas. These included the mermaid (whose legends were based upon distorted accounts of sea cows or dugongs and seals), the kraken (which owes its existence to exaggerated accounts of giant squids), and the sea serpent and sea monster. Pontoppidan makes a clear distinction between the "true" legless sea serpent and all the other monstrous creatures of the sea, like that of Hans Egede, which possessed "paws."

Pontoppidan collected and published a large number of previously unknown sea serpent reports. His book has become a basic source for those attempting to untangle the increasingly complex history of the sea serpent. The accounts the Bishop of Bergen collected were, as might be expected, a rather mixed lot. Some were second hand, and others so loaded with fabulous details that they are hard to take seriously. But there are also reports that come from eyewitnesses, who treat the subject soberly and modestly.

One tends to believe the statement of Captain Lorenz von Ferry who recounted for Pontoppidan how he shot at a large sea snake in August 1746. "As the snake swam faster than we could row, I took my gun, which was loaded with small shot, and fired at it; on this it immediately plunged under water. We rowed to the place where it sank down (which in the calm might be easily observed) and lay upon our oars, thinking it would come up again to the surface; however, it did not. Where the snake plunged down, the water appeared thick and red; perhaps the small shot might have wounded it, the distance being very little.

"The head of this sea serpent, which it held more than two feet above the surface of the water, resembled that of a horse. It was of a greyish colour, and the mouth was quite black, and very large. It had large black eyes, and a long white mane, which hung down to the surface of the water. Besides the head and neck we saw seven or eight folds, or coils, of this snake, which were very thick, and as far as we could guess there was a fathom's distance between each fold."

But eyewitness accounts, even the soberest and best of them, are not enough. Most scientists persisted in regarding the sea serpent as the result of a strange quirk of the Scandinavian mind. Then in 1808 something a good deal more substantial than a Scandinavian sailor's story turned up. It was a rotting carcass discovered on a beach at Stronsay in the Orkney Islands to the north of Scotland. Those who examined the carcass built up a picture of a serpentlike animal with a fringed back and—most incredibly—six little legs. Information on this curious carcass reached the Wernerian Natural History Society of Edinburgh, and the members were wild with a desire to get a look at it. But the Orkneys were hard to reach at the best of times, and it was already winter when the men in Edinburgh heard of the discovery. Before anyone with scientific training got a look at the carcass it was smashed to bits by a winter storm. However, some fragments of the skeleton were saved and promised to the Wernerian Society in time for the meeting at which the members planned to discuss the Stronsa beast. The fragments failed to arrive, but they had been examined in the Orkneys by one of the society's members, Dr. John Barclay. In January 1809, Dr. Barclay read an account of his observations on the Stronsa beast to the Wernerian Society. They were much impressed. The secretary of the society went so far as to say that this beast was certainly the creature described by Pontoppidan in his *Natural History of Norway.* The secretary proposed that the creature be named *Halsydrus Pontoppidani* (Pontoppidan's water snake).

But while Dr. Barclay's report said one thing, the drawings that he had made of the fragments from the Stronsa beast—some vertebrae, the cranium, the sternum, and a "fin"—gave a very different impression. These bones were quite clearly not the bones of a snake or any other reptile but those of a cartilaginous fish, probably some sort of large shark. We do not know whether the drawings were actually shown at the meeting or merely published later.

Information on the Stronsa beast also reached the hands of Everard Home, a London surgeon and naturalist who at that moment happened to be conducting a study of the huge but harmless basking shark *Squalus maximus.* From the drawings and descriptions Home concluded that the Stronsa beast was no unknown monster by rather a partially rotted large shark, most probably a basking shark. The measurement given for the Stronsa beast was fifty-five feet. Home believed this to be an exaggeration. The basking shark, as far as he knew, grew only to thirty feet. We now know that basking sharks grow to over forty feet, and may grow even larger.

The basking shark can rot in a curious way, making its carcass particularly prone to misidentification as a sea serpent. The gill apparatus decomposes first, and when it falls away it carries the shark's lower jaw with it. Thus the creature's most sharklike feature, its great gaping jaws, are not apparent on a rotting carcass. If the fins, or at least part of them, rot away, all that is left is thirty feet or so of flesh clinging to the backbone. If any of the lower fins do remain they are mistaken for legs.

To confuse identification further, when the creature's skin rots away, the surface muscles tend to break up into individual muscle fibers. When they dry out, these fibers resemble a stiff fur. The basking shark seems almost specially created to confuse the unwary. And carcasses of sea monsters from other parts of the world have usually turned out to be rotting sharks of one sort or another.

Home's conclusion about the Stronsa beast started a small but bitter scientific war between England and Scotland. Scots scientists defended the uniqueness of their Orkney monster with more nationalistic fervor than good sense. Finally in 1849 a well-known Edinburgh professor declared himself in favor of the basking shark hypothesis and the case of the Stronsa beast was at long last laid to rest.

Modern supporters of the sea serpent have been critical of Dr. Barclay and others who had supported the uniqueness of the Stronsa beast. Only fools, they declare, could have been fooled by such flimsy evidence. Yet there is certainly no reason to believe that the men who coined the name *Halsydrus Pontoppidani* were either blind or incompetent. They were merely wrong. Such ferocity from the monster buffs who should be most sympathetic to those who erred on the side of credulity is difficult to understand. One suspects that this attitude is due in part to nervousness. They seem to be trying to disassociate themselves from anyone who could make such a mistake. If they admit that good, honest, learned, and intelligent men like those of the Wernerian Natural History Society of Edinburgh can and often do make gross errors, they then might be forced to doubt some of the evidence in which they place so much faith.

Sea serpents had been reported off the American coast from time to time, but it was not until 1817 that there was a major sea serpent "flap" in America. In August of that year something that looked very like an enormous snake with a humped back was seen by many credible witnesses in and around Gloucester Harbor in Massachusetts. The Linnaean Society of New England quickly organized a committee to collect evidence from those who had caught sight of the creature.

The committee prepared a detailed set of questions to ask every witness, and committee members attempted to get statements from the witnesses as soon after the sighting as possible, so the information would be fresh. In short, they tried very hard to make a thorough and accurate investigation.

The monster was seen many times by many different persons during late 1817. The statements, while from persons of many different walks of life, all have a similarity of style, indicating that someone on the committee was editing them before they were published. But this seems to have resulted merely in a change of style rather than of substance. The reports presented a fairly consistent picture of a humped sea snake, perhaps a hundred feet long.

Traps and nets were set out to capture the creature, but they caught nothing. The Linnaeans theorized that the great sea snake had come so close inland in order to lay its eggs on shore, so they began a search for sea serpent eggs. They found no eggs but some boys brought them a three-foot-long, blackish snake with curious humps down its back. The boys had found the snake some fifty yards from the shore.

The members of the Linnaean Society's committee were completely convinced that the thing in Gloucester Harbor was a humped sea snake that had come in to lay eggs. Because of this strong conviction they committed a fantastic error which destroyed all their careful work, as far as the public was concerned. The committee decided that the three-foot humped snake was a baby sea serpent. The Linnaeans even named it *Scoliophis atlanticus* or the Atlantic Humped Snake. A report illustrated with excellent plates showing the bones and organs of the "baby sea serpent" appeared in the society's publication. The report noted that the humped sea serpent was closely related to the common black snake (*Coluber constrictor*).

"On the whole, as these two animals agree in so many conspicuous, important and peculiar characteristics, and as no material difference between them has yet been clearly pointed out, excepting that of size, the Society will probably feel justified in considering them individuals of the same species . . ."

It never seemed to occur to anyone in the society that the "baby sea serpent" *was* a common black snake, and that the humps along its back were an abnormal condition, the result of injury or disease. This obvious conclusion was quickly pointed out by the French scientist Alexandre Lesueur after he read the society's report. Lesueur's criticism was so telling that the Linnaean Society of New England retired from the sea serpent business in shock and silence.

This hasty withdrawal in the face of the criticism from France was understandable but unfortunate. The Linnaeans had conducted an admirable investigation of the strange sightings in Gloucester Harbor. The statements of the witnesses were and still are valuable. The black snake blunder did not disprove the existence of a sea serpent in Gloucester Harbor. Even Lesueur pointed this out, and said that if the giant humped snake reappeared he would travel to America to see it.

But after the black snake fiasco in New England, the sea serpent slipped even lower in public esteem. People who saw strange animals in the sea no longer rushed forth to identify them as sea serpents. There is a story, perhaps apocryphal, that a ship's crew sighted a sea serpent and called down to their captain, who was below deck at the time, to come up and see it. He refused and later said, "Had I said I had seen the sea serpent I should have been considered to be a warranted liar my life after."

The next major event in the history of the sea serpent was also not a particularly happy one. In 1845 the skeleton of a 114-foot-long sea serpent was exhibited on Broadway by the famous fossil collector Dr. Albert Koch, who had already made so many remarkable discoveries of fossil animals in America. Koch is an enigma. He was a fossil hunter of great skill and talent, but his love of sensation, and probably money, overwhelmed any passion he might have had for scientific exactitude. Koch came to America from Germany with the apparently self-conferred title of doctor and a considerable knowledge of fossils. In 1840 he found a cache of mastodon bones on the banks of a river in Missouri. This was a respectable find, but an ordinary one. The American mastodon was already well known. So Koch rearranged the bones. He put the creature's great curving tusks on top of the skull so they looked like great curving horns. He then threw in a few extra bones that he happened to find, and he declared the concoction to be *Missourium* (the Missouri animal) and the largest fossil mammal ever found.

Missourium was fairly well received, even by professional

paleontologists. But some wondered about the rather unusual way in which the bones had been put together. They assumed that "Doctor Koch" would correct these errors in due time. It seemed an honest mistake, for strange reconstructions were quite common in those early days of paleontology. Koch sold *Missourium* for a considerable sum to the British Museum. They managed to salvage a very good mastadon skeleton from it.

Encouraged by this easy success, Koch next excavated a collecton of bones that he declared to be behemoth of the Bible. These were sold to Frederick William IV of Prussia. But Koch's crowning glory was the Great Sea Serpent, which, with characteristic bravado, he also declared to be leviathan of the Bible. Koch gave his sea serpent a Latin scientific name —*Hydrarchos sillimani*—Silliman's water king. Benjamin Silliman was a professor at Yale. Only a silly man can believe in *Hydrarchos sillimani* became a popular gibe. Silliman was not pleased with the honor and forced Koch to withdraw the name. Koch changed his monster's title to *Hydrarchos harlani*, in honor of Dr. Richard Harlan, a pioneer American paleontologist, who had once praised Koch's work but had since died. Koch's creature, by whatever name, was still a fake, or at least a patently and deliberately false reconstruction.

But in a sense the bones Koch put on display were those of a real sea monster. In Alabama he had discovered a virtual treasure trove of bones belonging to the extinct whale *Zeuglodon*. In life *Zeuglodon* had a pointed snout, huge mouth filled with wicked-looking teeth, and an elongated sixty-foot body. The creature was already well known to science at the time Koch made his Alabama find. Modern reconstructions show *Zeulogdon* to be the image of a sea serpent, and many monster buffs believe that some form of surviving *Zeuglodon* really is the Great Sea Serpent. Even if this *Zeuglodon* theory ultimately turns out to be true, Koch cannot be exonerated, for he deliberately joined together all the *Zeulogdon* vertebrae he could find, in order to get a skeleton long enough and serpentine enough to satisfy the sensation seekers. A couple of large shells were appended to the monster as paddles. By 1845 Koch's weakness for bizarre reconstructions was already well known, and his sea serpent was a short-lived sensation.

After such a string of well-publicized blunders and hoaxes, you can see why it was difficult for anyone to take the sea serpent very seriously. Then came 1848 and the report of Captain M'Quhae of the *Daedalus*, and public opinion was turned around once more.

Of course not everyone, not even in Great Britain, was won over to the cause of the sea serpent out of respect for the good sense and good sight of British naval officers. Leader of the anti-sea serpent faction was Sir Richard Owen, an anatomist and then curator of the Hunterian Museum. A little later Owen became even more famous for his opposition to something else—the theory of evolution. He was Darwin's bitterest enemy and, as Darwin later confessed, the only one who ever annoyed him. Monster buffs love to link Owen's opposition to evolution to his opposition to the sea serpent, and conclude, rather illogically, that since evolution has been proved the sea serpent exists.

There could be no denying that Owen was a man of enormous learning. But in an argument he was arrogant, dictatorial, bombastic, insulting, and often dishonest. He displayed just about every trait destined to gain sympathy for his opponent. To turn an old saying around, with enemies like this, the sea serpent needed no friends. Owen usually based his arguments on the premise that those who had observed the sea serpent were not trained scientists and therefore not competent to judge what they had seen.

Owen theorized that the men of the *Daedalus* had really

Alexander the Great battling monsters. Drawing from a fifteenth-century version of the Alexander legend.

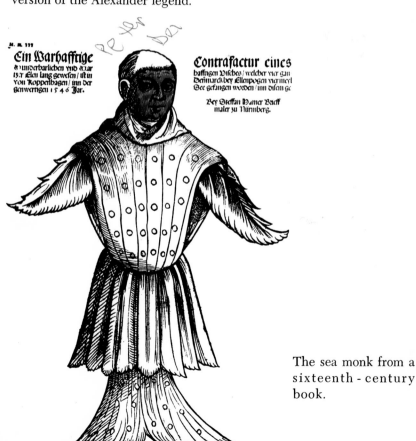

The sea monk from a sixteenth - century book.

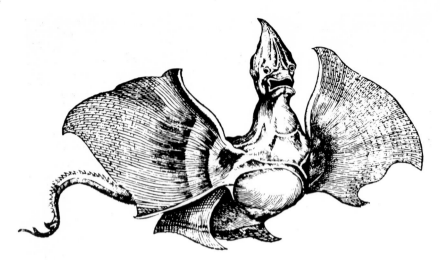

A Jenny Haniver dragon made out of a skate or ray.

Aldrovandi's two-legged winged dragon.

Albrecht Dürer's engraving of St. Michael fighting the Dragon of the Apocalypse.

Two animals who may have contributed to the dragon legend, the flying lizard *Draco volans* and the python.

The whale according to Olaus Magnus.

The sea serpent according to Olaus Magnus.

The *Daedlaus* sea serpent. Could it have been a wandering canoe?

One of the sea serpents described by Bishop Erik Pontoppidan.

A sketch of a sea serpent sighted off Galveston, Texas.

Associated Newspapers Ltd.

The famous London surgeon's photograph of the Loch Ness Monster.

World Book Encyclopedia

Photo taken in 1955 near Urquhart Castle ruins at Loch Ness by P. A. MacNab. Top of tower is sixty-four feet above water level, and can be compared to the size of the "thing" in the water.

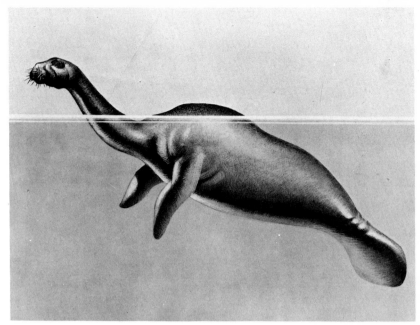

Hypothetical sirenian or member of the sea cow family, according to Dr. Roy P. Mackal of the University of Chicago. Dr. Mackal thinks such a creature might account for the Loch Ness sightings. The largest known sirenian, Steller's sea cow, grew to a length of thirty-five feet.

Clem Lister Skelton, full-time watcher at Loch Ness.

Alex Campbell, the man who named the monster.

F.W. "Ted" Holiday, propounder of the "Great Orm" theory.

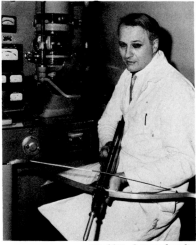

World Book Encyclopedia

Dr. Roy P. Mackal, with crossbow for monster hunting.

Medieval conception of the wild man.

European play with wild man character. Engraving by Pieter Brueghel.

Paintings from the Schloss Ambras, Innsbruck, Austria, reproduced courtesy of Dr. Gerald P. Hodge.

Engraving by Stefano della Bella, Yale University Art Gallery, Edward B. Greene Fund.

The hairy Gonzalis family.

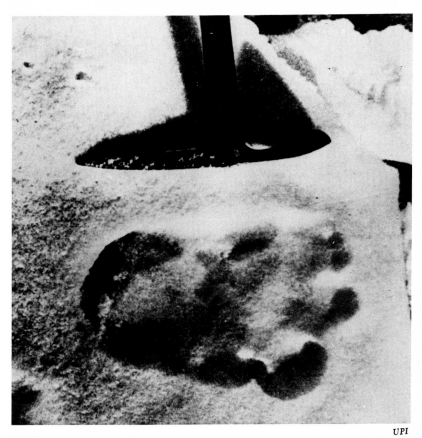

Mountaineer Eric Shipton's photograph of the "footprint of a yeti."
Print is compared in size to the head of an ice ax.

Still from film taken by Roger Patterson supposedly showing America's Abominable Snowman in the woods northeast of Eureka, California. Patterson estimated the creature to be about seven and a half feet high.

Early drawings of dinosaurs and giant sea reptiles make them look like dragons and sea monsters.

The Coelacanth, a real living fossil.

The woolly mammoth. Could they still survive in the arctic?

seen a sea elephant or some other type of large seal. "It is very probable," he wrote to the *Times,* "that no one on board the *Daedalus* ever before beheld a gigantic seal freely swimming in the open ocean." That was not a tactful thing to say.

Owen's "solution" to the *Daedalus* mystery was printed in the *Times,* and a few days later the *Times* also printed an icy response from Captain M'Quhae. The gist of the captain's defense was that he damn well knew a seal or sea elephant when he saw one. He also pointed to several examples of how Owen had shamelessly misinterpreted the *Daedalus* report in order to make it fit his own theory.

By the end of the nineteenth century the Great Sea Serpent was ready for its first major biographer since Bishop Pontoppidan. The man was Antoon Cornelis Oudemans, a Dutch biologist and expert on ticks and mites. Perhaps as a relief from the study of these tiny pests, Dr. Oudemans turned to collecting information about the great unknown giant of the sea. Unlike Owen, who was determined to find ordinary explanations for sea serpent sightings, Oudemans was convinced that most of them were genuine, and that there really was a large unknown sea creature. His great task was to determine the nature of the beast.

After collecting and analyzing an impressive number of reports, Oudemans came to the surprising conclusion that the Great Sea Serpent was no serpent at all but some sort of gigantic long-necked seal with small flippers. Although a mammal, Oudemans' sea serpent resembled in an extraordinary way the group of reptiles called *plesiosaurs* from the age of the dinosaurs. Thus what had begun in antiquity as a gigantic water snake became, in the view of its leading nineteenth-century supporter, an elongated seal.

Oudemans' major reason for rejecting the reptiles in favor of the mammals was the apparent world-wide distribution of the monster. It seemed to pop up everywhere and was particularly active in far northern waters, which were much too cold for a reptile. Other characteristics in the mammal's favor were the often-mentioned smooth skin, which could have been slick seal-like fur, whiskers, and a mane.

Oudemans had set an enormous task for himself. He had to account for a large number of often contradictory characteristics. Witnesses reported seeing sea serpents with manes and without manes, with whiskers and without whiskers, with humps and without humps, and so on. Oudemans had to do a great deal of pushing and hauling with the facts to get all these contradictions within a single species. The result was a rickety and often quite ridiculous theoretical super-structure. The *Times* chided his book as "a cumbrous and elaborate, albeit quite unconscious joke." Other critics were even less kind. But the reaction of the scientific community was not entirely negative. Some praised his courage in tackling this controversial subject even if they did not subscribe to his opinions.

Meanwhile, the sea serpent, quite unaware of the controversy which swirled about it on the land, kept popping up here and there in the sea. Dr. Oudemans' book had just been published when the *Umfuli* steaming southward toward the Cape of Good Hope encountered what was first described as "a Monster Fish of the Serpent shape." The encounter was not appreciated by the ship's commander Captain R. J. Cringle. Thirty-five years later Captain Cringle claimed that he had suffered so much ridicule for his story that he no longer wished to talk about it. Yet talk he did:

"It was rushing through the water at great speed, and was throwing water from its breast as a vessel throws water from her bows. I saw full 15 feet of its head and neck on three separate occasions . . . The body was all the time visible . . . the base or body, from which the neck sprang, was much thicker than the neck itself, and I should not, therefore, call it a serpent. Had it been breezy enough to ruffle the water, or hazy I should have had some doubt about the creature; but the sea being so perfectly smooth, I had not the slightest doubt in my mind as to its being a sea monster . . . this thing, whatever it was, was in sight for over half an hour. In fact, we did not lose sight of it until darkness came on."

Captain Cringle's account was confirmed by several passengers aboard the *Umfuli*. The captain grumpily insisted that what he saw was not an island of sea weed, a string of porpoises, or any of the other things critics told him he had seen.

Sir Richard Owen often complained that the sea serpent was always sighted by sailors and never by scientists or trained naturalists. This was hardly surprising since sailors spend much more time looking at the sea than scientists do. But in 1905 even that criticism was swept away. Two British naturalists and fellows of the Zoological Society, E. G. B. Meade-Waldo and M. J. Nicoll, were on a scientific cruise aboard the yacht *Valhalla*. About fifteen miles off the coast of Brazil their attention was called to a strange object in the sea.

According to Meade-Waldo: "I looked and immediately saw a large fin or frill sticking out of the water, dark seaweed-brown in colour, somewhat crinkled at the edge. It was apparently about 6 feet in length, and projected from 18 inches to 2 feet from the water.

"I got my field-glasses on to it (a powerful pair of Goertz-Trieder), and almost as soon as I had them on the frill, a great head and neck rose out of the water in front of the frill; the neck did not touch the frill in the water, but came out of the water in front of it, at a distance of certainly not less than 18 inches, probably more. The neck appeared about the thickness of a slight man's body, and from 7 to 8 feet out of the water; head and neck were all about the same thickness.

"The head had a very turtle-like appearance, as had also the eye. I could see the line of the mouth, but we were sailing pretty fast, and quickly drew away from the object, which was going very slowly. It moved its head and neck from side to side in a pecular manner; The colour of the head and neck was dark brown above, and whitish below—almost white, I think."

Nicoll gave essentially the same account of the sighting, adding his belief that the creature had been a mammal not a reptile. "It is, of course, impossible to be certain of this, but the general appearance of the creature, especially the soft, almost rubber-like fin, gave one this impression."

The years between the publication of Oudemans' book and the outbreak of World War I were the golden age of the sea serpent. Not that it was seen more often, or that the sightings were any better, but each sighting got more and better publicity. The public as well as many scientists and naturalists began to treat the sea serpent with respect. It seemed only a matter of time until the creature was conclusively identified a long last.

But with the outbreak of World War I sailors lost interest in looking for sea serpents. They had to watch out for U-boats, which were far more dangerous than even the most ferocious of Olaus Magnus' sailor-snatching sea serpents. Occasionally even the Great Sea Serpent or at least some sort of sea monster fell victim to a U-boat attack.

U-boat Captain Georg Gunther Freiherr von Forstner reported that in 1915 he sank the British steamer *Iberian.* Shortly after the ship went down there was a violent underwater explosion and among the objects thrown to the surface was a violently struggling sea monster. Von Forstner described the monster as looking like a sixty-foot crocodile with a long neck.

This incident is notable because it is one of the very few

times a sea monster was reported being observed in its entirety. It is also notable because von Forstner has some glaring contradictions in his story and the whole thing is, unfortunately, highly suspect.

After the war the sea serpent never seemed to regain its previous popularity. People were disappointed with it and bored by it. Once having committed themselves to belief in the sea serpent they expected quick and conclusive proof of its existence, or at least some new and sensational sightings. When nothing was forthcoming except the same old unsatisfactory observations which had been collected for so long, faith and interest began to weaken.

A brief flurry of enthusiasm was kicked up in 1930 by a book called *The Case for the Sea Serpent,* written by Lieutenant Commander Rupert T. Gould. Gould was a retired naval officer, radio broadcaster, and a tireless collector of odd and unexplained phenomena. His book was aggressively partisan toward the existence of the sea serpent. In many of his conclusions Gould had jumped far, far beyond the facts at hand. Yet he had conscientiously collected and documented a large number of previously unpublished sea serpent sightings.

But people were hungry for new sensations and when in 1933 the first reports of the Loch Ness monster began appearing in the press, they quickly captured the public's attention and this fresh-water monster soon displaced the sea serpent as the world's number one unknown animal. It might be more accurate to say that the sea serpent was simply transferred to Loch Ness, for everyone assumed that the Loch Ness monster and the sea serpent were one and the same. For years people persisted in ignoring the quite obvious fact that there is no possible way by which a large aquatic animal could travel between the open sea and the waters of Loch Ness. But with its long neck, small head, and humped back the

Loch Ness monsters seemed remarkably like the traditional sea serpent.

From Holland old Dr. Oudemans thundered for the Loch Ness monster's blood. He hoped it would, at long last, provide confirmation for his disputed thesis of the sea serpent. He urged the British public not to be tenderhearted but to kill the monster "for science."

While the Loch Ness monster has been reportedly photographed, filmed, and tracked with sonar, the search for the Great Sea Serpent has continued in its old desultory way, being bumped along by random sightings of inconclusive quality. Then in 1964 the first photographs of the sea serpent were reportedly taken. The photos, in glorious color, were shot off the coast of Australia by Robert Le Serrac, a globe-trotting French photographer. The sea serpent these photos showed, was far from traditional. It seemed to be swimming, or rather resting in shallow water, and looked more like a gigantic tadpole than anything else.

Bernard Heuvelmans was asked his opinion of the photos. He had strong doubts but said that if they were not a hoax, then they probably showed some sort of giant eel-shaped member of the shark family, previously unknown to science.

Le Serrac said that he had also taken motion pictures of the monster. These would be far more conclusive, and much harder to fake. But when the film failed to show up in France for examination Heuvelmans became even more suspicious. He did some checking into the photographer's background. In the stories which accompanied the photos, Le Serrac was described as a man who "inspires confidence." But Heuvelmans found that he was actually being sought by Interpol for skipping out of France and leaving behind a long string of unpaid bills. Even the yacht in which Le Serrac had sailed to Australia in search of the sea serpent had been attached

by his creditors before the voyage, and he was using it il-
legally.

An even more damaging bit of evidence was uncovered by
Heuvelmans. Before he sailed, Le Serrac had attempted to
get some people to share the expenses of his expedition. He
promised them a good return on their investment, for the
voyage would net a lot of money. "It's to do with the sea
serpent," he said.

When Le Serrac returned to France he was sent to prison.
Even while he was behind bars the sea serpent photos he had
taken were still being published in various magazines as the
genuine article, and the photographer himself being described
as a man who inspires confidence. Moreover, the stories continued to say that scientists had affirmed that the photos
were those of a real sea monster. For several years agencies
continued to peddle the photos as genuine, and for all I know
they are still being sold today.

This rather dismal little episode has no real significance in
the history of the sea serpent, for photographic faking has
played almost no part in the growth of the sea serpent legend,
although it has been quite important in some other monster
legends. The case for the reality of the sea serpent is impressive enough without the Le Serrac photos. The story is recounted as a warning to all who are inclined to swallow the
sensational monster "revelations" of the sort that seem to appear with depressing regularity in fairly reputable magazines.
Not that most magazines would actually concoct a hoax or
print a story that they knew for certain was false. But the
thought of a healthy boost in circulation will tempt many
editors to close their eyes to suspicious elements or even glaring contradictions in a story. Many monster buffs will do the
same sort of thing, but they at least have the excuse of being
true believers.

While most people had either decided that the sea serpent

did not exist at all, or did not care whether or not it existed, Bernard Heuvelmans toiled patiently away, checking out all possible information on the sea serpent. In 1968, after nearly a decade of what he described as "the hardest work I have ever done," Heuvelmans' opus, *In the Wake of Sea Serpents,* was published.

Heuvelmans reviews all the classic cases cited by Oudemans, Gould, and others, and brings the catalog of sea serpent events up to date. But Heuvelmans is no mere collector. In his final chapter, "Disentangled and Classified at Last," he attempts to determine the kind of creature or creatures that were responsible for the legend of the Great Sea Serpent. While Oudemans tried to attribute all sea serpent sightings to a single long-necked mammal, Heuvelmans does the opposite, indeed, one may say he goes to the other extreme. He postulates nine different sorts of large unknown sea animals, five giant mammals, two huge reptiles, a colossal eel, and something called the Yellow-belly which is of an unknown type. In practice he is willing to drop two of the nine, one of the reptiles and the Yellow-belly, for the reports concerning them he believes are too infrequent and too vague to inspire much confidence. But he sticks by the other seven: the long-necked sea serpent, the many-humped sea serpent, the many-finned sea serpent, the merhorse, and the super otter—all mammals—plus the super eel and the reptilian marine saurian.

Oudemans floundered upon getting us to believe that so many different characteristics could be displayed by a single animal. Heuvelmans must make us believe that there are not one or two but a veritable zoo full of large unknown and very unique-looking creatures swimming around in the sea.

Now the seas are wide and deep, and there is a great deal we do not know about them, but is it possible that we have overlooked all of these different kinds of animals? It seems hard to believe. It is particularly hard to believe because the majority of Heuvelmans' theoretical sea serpents are mammals. Of all creatures mammals should be the most obvious and easy to identify. They are air breathers and must come to the surface frequently. Many basically marine mammals like seals spend much of their time on land. Mammals are intelligent and curious; therefore, they should show more interest in passing ships than the sea serpent seems to. An anatomical objection is that while most marine mammals, whales, seals, sea cows, and the like tend to have torpedo shapes and necks that are either severely reduced or entirely absent, at least some of Heuvelmans' theoretical mammalian sea serpents have very long necks.

We must recall that the evidence for the existence of a large and unknown serpentiform animal in the sea rests entirely on reported sightings. Not a single one of these creatures, as far as we know, has even been washed ashore or photographed. This in itself does not destroy the case, but it is something to think about.

I guess our belief or nonbelief in the sea serpent rests not on the probability of such a creature existing, for no one can really determine such probabilities. It rests on our attitude toward man as an observer and interpreter of the world around him. Could an experienced seafarer like Captain M'Quhae and some of his equally experienced officers actually have mistaken a dugout canoe for a living creature? Of course they couldn't, say the buffs, and perhaps the buffs are correct. But mistakes of vision at sea are incredibly common and often very convincing.

At the end of the last century the French frigate *La Belle Poule* was searching for a missing ship. The watch signaled that he saw a disabled vessel, and in broad daylight the entire crew of the frigate stared off into the distance where they saw a raft and several boats crowded with men. Only when a boat was sent out from the frigate to the aid of the survivors did the men of *La Belle Poule* discover that what they had seen was nothing more than a few floating branches and trees.

One final thought, if Oudemans and Heuvelmans are correct, and the sea serpent really is a huge and unknown marine mammal or mammals, perhaps it is best that we do not believe in them, that we continue to consider them something legendary and laughable. Man's record regarding the preservation of other species, particularly species of marine mammals, is disgraceful. We have virtually exterminated several species of whales and seals, and we have exterminated the giant sea cow. Is there any guarantee that we would behave any better toward the sea serpent, which if it exists at all is clearly a rare animal?

I have visions of oceanographic ships of a dozen nations pursuing the creatures in order to obtain a sufficient number of stuffed specimens to satisfy national pride. One can see a thriving black market in sea serpent specimens, or envision rich "sportsmen" outfitting expensive expeditions so that they can have the glory of killing one of the remaining sea serpents. The slaughter would probably make the pages of some "outdoor" magazines. When it was too late marine biologists and others would gather and somberly announce that if all this wanton destruction didn't stop the sea serpent would soon be extinct. What a fate, to be discovered just in time to be hunted to extinction! It has all happened before, and is still happening today. No, far better that the sea serpent remain a legend until such time as man realizes that the world was not made solely for his exploitation.

Until such a time, I, for one, am ready to laugh very loudly at the next sea serpent tale I hear, whether I believe it or not.

Nessie and Her Brood

Each nation had its own conception of evil spirits or monsters that lived in deep lakes. In the Highlands of Scotland, the monstrous inhabitants of lakes (or lochs) were called "water horses" or "water bulls." There was hardly a loch or bay which, according to local folklore, did not have some sort of monster in it.

But the Loch Ness monster has a better pedigree than most of the other Scottish lake monsters. While most were only known in oral tradition, the Loch Ness monster was mentioned in writing in A.D. 565. The monster, it seems, ran afoul of the great Scottish holy man, Saint Columba. Adamnan, Saint Columba's biographer, tells of an incident where the saint saved a swimmer from the rampaging monster by saying, "Think not to go further, touch not thou that man. Quick! Go back! Then the beast, upon hearing the voice of the saint, was terrified and fled backwards more rapidly than he came."

It was traditional in pagan societies for heroes to slay

dragons and other monsters. When the pagans became Christians these monster-fighting activities were often taken over by the saints. The story of Saint Columba and the Loch Ness monster would have remained nothing more than an obscure bit of folklore, to be treated no more seriously than the story of Saint George and the dragon, had it not been for the events of 1933–1934.

During those years a road was built around the once-isolated loch in the Highlands. The construction brought a large number of outsiders to Loch Ness, and clearing the shore of the loch for the road gave observers a better view of the water. In those years the Loch Ness monster appeared, or reappeared, if we are to accept the story of Saint Columba.

The Loch Ness monster captured the public fancy as no creature real or imaginary has in a very long time. It knocked the Great Sea Serpent right out of contention as the number one unknown animal in the world. To this day, despite years of disappointment, the Loch Ness monster remains the world's most popular monster, and the only one for which there is a regular and well-organized search.

So much has already been written on the Loch Ness monster that it seems unnecessary to give another detailed account of its history. A brief rundown of background information will be supplied but we will concentrate on developments in the story of the monster during the last few years.

Of the thousands who have reported seeing the monster since 1933 the vast majority have seen only its back or "humps." Most commonly what they have seen is a shape in the water that looks something like an upturned boat, or a string of them. This shape may be anywhere from a few inches to many feet above the water.

Only a small number have reported actually seeing the creature's head and neck. One of the first people to sight the creature's head, and indeed the man who claims to have

coined the term Loch Ness monster, is Alex Campbell, a retired fisheries official at the loch. He saw the monster for the
first time in 1934. "It had a long tapering neck, about six feet
long, and a smallish head, with a serpentine look about it,
and a huge hump behind which I reckon was about thirty
feet long. It was turning its head constantly."

In addition to his duty at the loch, Campbell was also a
correspondent for the Inverness *Courier,* the local newspaper
for the region. It was Campbell's reports that helped catapult
the Loch Ness monster to world-wide fame. Why did he call
it monster? "Not bcause there was anything horrible about
it at all, but because of the great size of the creature."

The serpentine appearance of the monster's head and neck
was firmly fixed in the public's consciousness by "the famous
London surgeon's photograph." It was taken in 1934 by Kenneth Wilson, a surgeon on holiday in Scotland. The photo
apparently shows the snakelike neck and tiny head of the
monster sticking out of the waters of the loch.

In the 1930s most people agreed that the monster looked
very much like an ancient marine reptile plesiosaur. At the
time the plesiosaur was also a popular candidate for the
Great Sea Serpent, and so was very much on everyone's mind.

After the first sensational sightings there were no further
important revelations about the monster. The skeptics and the
jokers began to move in. By the beginning of World War II
(during which time it dropped out of the news entirely) the
Loch Ness monster came to be regarded as either a hoax
concocted by canny Scots hotel owners or a hallucination
seen only by those who imbibed too freely in Scotland's most
famous product.

But a hardy few kept the faith. After the war they came
back to Loch Ness and in the face of scorn and ridicule managed to collect what has to be considered the best evidence
for the existence of any monster anywhere in the world.

Exhibit A in the new case for the Loch Ness monster is the Dinsdale film. In 1960 monster watcher and amateur photographer Tim Dinsdale filmed what he thought to be the monster swimming in the far side of the loch.

To the untrained observer the short film shows little—just a spot moving through the water. It could be anything—a motorboat, for example. That is what many viewers claimed, and still claim the film shows. In 1965 David James, a former Member of Parliament who had become interested in the Loch Ness "problem," persuaded photographic interpretation experts at the Royal Air Force to examine the Dinsdale film. On the basis of an exhaustive frame-by-frame analysis the RAF reported that the shape in the film is "probably an animate object." Furthermore, they speculated that the object might be as much as ninety-two feet in length although it was probably more like thirty or forty feet long and "not less than six feet wide and five feet high." It was also moving through the water at a considerable speed.

Since Dinsdale took his film other films have been taken, all at long range. One apparently shows the humps of two monsters moving side by side through the water. Another supposedly shows the monster on a small pebbly beach at the loch. The problem with these films, as with the Dinsdale film, is that they are unspectacular. The object that is supposed to be the monster appears as nothing more than a little blob. Despite the RAF report many refuse to consider the case for the Loch Ness monster proven. They contend, quite correctly, that photographic interpretation, even when done by experts, is far from an exact science. The quality of the monster films is so poor that even the experts might easily be wrong.

Public interest in the monster was beginning to wane again until 1968, when it received a new lease on life. Scientists from the University of Birmingham (England) using a new type of sonar equipment picked up stirrings in Loch Ness that seemed highly suggestive. (The tests were made in 1967 but the results were not published until the following year.) The conclusions drawn from the tests were highly tentative. Wrote Hugh Braithwaite who headed the expedition: "Since the objects . . . are clearly comprised of animals, is it possible they could be fish? The high rate of ascent and descent makes it seem very unlikely, and fishery biologists we have consulted cannot suggest what fish they might be. It is a temptation to suppose they must be the fabulous Loch Ness monsters, now observed for the first time in their underwater activities! The present data, while leaving this a possibility, are quite inadequate to decide the matter. A great deal of further investigation with more refined equipment— which is not at present available—is needed before definite conclusions can be drawn."

But even this cautious approach was quickly challenged by other scientists who said what the sonar had picked up was a "ghost" not a monster. The University of Birmingham equipment, they said, was registering a false image, a not uncommon occurrence with sonar.

Naturally, during this period the Loch Ness monster, or Nessie, as she, he, it, or they is affectionately called by the watchers, has not gone unnoticed. Aside from the tourists who flock by the hundreds each summer to the shores of Loch Ness to see if they can catch a glimpse of the elusive creature, there has been, since 1963, a regular yearly expedition organized to watch for the monster. The expedition is run by the Loch Ness Phenomena Investigation Bureau, Ltd.* founded by David James. During the warmer months a full crew of watchers, armed with binoculars and cameras, drive specially equipped vans to various locations around the loch. On a good day they have virtually the entire surface of Loch Ness under visual observation. Most of the watchers are student

* The Loch Ness Investigation Bureau Limited is a non-profit organization.

volunteers from various countries. (America is most heavily represented.) Two weeks of monster watching makes a cheap and often exciting holiday. But it would be a mistake to underestimate either the seriousness or competence of these amateurs. The Bureau is a non-profit organization.

Field Director of the Loch Ness Investigation is Clem Skelton, a photographer with a severe case of monster fever. During the long Highland winter, when the weather becomes frigid and the daylight almost negligible, and the tourists and college students abandon the shores of Loch Ness, Skelton and his wife remain in their trailer on the shores of the loch. Their closest neighbor may be the monster itself.

Since he spends more time looking for the monster than anyone else, Skelton has quite naturally seen the monster or what he thinks is the monster more times than anyone else.

Once, he says, he was practically on top of it. In June 1964 Skelton saw the creature's hump from a distance of only fifteen yards. "I was rowing a boat across the loch at 12:30 A.M. It never really gets dark at Loch Ness in the middle of June, there is always a glow in the sky. I looked over my right shoulder and there it was. It was the classic upturned boat sighting, but it was bigger than my boat and if anyone wanted to win the diamond skulls at Henley he should have rowed nearly as fast as I did to get out of its way."

Skelton is absolutely convinced that there is a monster in Loch Ness. Many others who have seen what they take to be the monster are equally convinced, as are a lot of people who have never seen the monster at all. Each year the Loch Ness Investigation carefully records all the sightings. From their lists they try to eliminate all hoaxes and mistakes. Skelton figures that eighty to ninety percent of the people who think they have seen the monster have really seen something else. The remaining probable sightings are then carefully tallied and published by the Bureau at the end of the year. They make an impressive record. But the monster watchers know that they need more than an endless accumulation of sighting reports to convince the scientific world and the public at large that Nessie exists.

Numerous suggestions have been made for catching the monster, from poisoning the loch to stretching a net across it. Less drastic but more practical suggestions have been offered for getting a piece of the monster's hide (or whatever) by the use of a harpoon or crossbow. In 1962 a small ship sailed around Loch Ness with a crew member on deck, ready with a long pole tipped with a piece of sticky stuff. The hope was that with the pole and sticky material they could detach a scale or piece of skin from the monster. The problem was that in order to stick, or shoot, or prod the monster you have to get close to it. In this the monster has proved thoroughly uncooperative.

Most hopes are pinned on getting what members of the Bureau call "The Picture"—a good closeup shot, or preferably film of the monster with its head above the water. This, they feel, unlike the vague spots and shapes which have appeared in the other pictures, would clinch the case for the monster. For this reason they have spent the bulk of their funds, which come from private donations and grants, on buying good camera equipment. The largest single grant, twenty thousand dollars, came from Field Educational Enterprises, the same organization that helped to bankroll an expedition to find the Abominable Snowman in the Himalayas.

The Loch Ness monster is a near-perfect subject for scientific investigation. Unlike the Great Sea Serpent, which could be anywhere in the vast expanse or abyssal depths of the oceans, the Loch Ness monster is strictly confined. No large creature could get in or out of Loch Ness without being observed. So whatever it is lives in the loch and has for a long time. Naturally the monster buffs do not say what they are seeing is the same ageless specimen confronted by Saint Columba a millennium ago. They speak of the loch at home for a small but viable breeding herd of monsters.

Many people wonder why, if the monster's range is so confined, a specimen has not yet been captured or at least photographed at closer range. The question is a good one. But just because the monster has not yet been captured or well photographed, we should not simply jump to the conclusion that it does not exist. Loch Ness is a lot bigger than it looks on the map. It is the largest body of fresh water in the British Isles, cutting twenty-four miles through Scotland's Great Glen. At one end it is connected to the sea by the little river Ness. It also serves as a link in the Caledonian Canal which bisects the Highlands and is the country's principal waterway.

The waters of Loch Ness are deep, dark, cold, and often dangerous. Average width of the loch is only a mile, but the sides plunge precipitously to depths of over seven hundred feet. A suspension of peat makes the water brown and murky and the few divers who have ventured into it found themselves in a world where even a strong light would penetrate no more than twelve feet. The loch never freezes, but it never really warms up either. Throughout the year the temperature hovers in the chilly mid-forties. Currents of surprising strength can catch the unwary boater, and more than one has rowed or sailed onto the loch and never been seen again.

Because of the dangers of the loch, the history of the monster has been kept remarkably free from a particular sort of hoax—the kind in which a group of jokers float a model monster in the water. The model would have to be propelled in some way, presumably by a swimmer or a group of swimmers underwater. It would then have to be pulled under or gotten out of sight in some other way, before the startled observers had a chance to discover what it really was. But nobody wants to go swimming in Loch Ness, particularly underwater. A group of college students who built a rubber monster were forced to float it in a smaller, friendlier loch nearby.

Divers don't like to go into the loch at all. When they do they can't see much anyway. So there is little point in searching for the monster underwater, except by sonar.

You might think that with all the publicity the monster has received in the last decade the shores of Loch Ness would be packed solidly with tourists bristling with binoculars and cameras and that the boats would be as thick as rowboats in the Central Park lagoon. Actually, even at the peak of the tourist season Loch Ness seems pleasantly uncrowded to an American. There are relatively few good places to sit and watch for the monster, and the weather is so rotten so often that only the most dedicated will brave it regularly. Boats are surprisingly infrequent on the loch, and if you wished to rent one you would find them scarce.

Despite all the publicity, the search for the Loch Ness monster remains remarkably underfinanced. Visitors to the loch often ask expedition members why they don't just send down a miniature submarine to find the monster—as if miniature submarines were the cheapest and most easily obtainable things in the world. The Loch Ness investigators have never had anywhere near the amount of funds they need to conduct a thorough investigation.

In 1969 a miniature submarine actually was brought to the loch to aid in the investigation. But the submarine was a homemade contraption, and it never worked properly. Despite high hopes it added nothing to our knowledge of the Loch Ness monster.

Therefore, it is possible—barely perhaps—but possible, that a large unknown creature or rather a group of them really do live in the depths of Loch Ness and have escaped conclusive detection.

Let us assume for the moment that there really is a monster in Loch Ness. What is the nature of the beast? This sort of speculation is a favorite topic of discussion among monster watchers and opinions have followed the fashions of the time. When the Loch Ness monster first became famous in the early 1930s the most popular idea was that the creature was a member of a group of giant aquatic reptiles called plesiosaurs or something very much like them.

In 1934 Mr. Arthur Grant of Drumnadrochit, a small town on the shores of Loch Ness, thought he saw the monster on the road at night in the light of his motorcycle. When asked to produce a picture of what he saw he drew what looked like a simplified plesiosaur—long neck, narrow body, four small legs and long tail.

Today the plesiosaur theory is very much out of fashion among monster buffs. Somewhere along the line someone realized that the plesiosaur, being a reptile, was cold-blooded —or more accurately lacked internal temperature controls. Thus, the cold waters of Loch Ness would simply be too cold an environment to support a reptile.

Such reasoning, however, seems rather unimaginative for a group that is used to a great deal of unbridled speculation. In the first place, reptiles can tolerate greater variations in temperature than most people imagine. Still, no small modern reptile could live and remain active in the waters of Loch Ness year round. But the plesiosaur was neither small nor modern.

The larger the reptile, the better control it has over its internal temperature. It takes longer for a large alligator to heat up and cool down than it does for a small lizard. Edwin H. Colbert of the American Museum of Natural History has speculated that because of their great size the dinosaurs may have been able to maintain a fairly constant internal temperature.

Says Colbert: "It may be that the dinosaurs were so successful for so many million years because so many of them were giants, and because as giants they had the advantages of fairly constant body temperatures, and correlatively of fairly constant rates of body metabolism. This is something to think about."

Not even the wildest Loch Ness monster story has the creature rivaling one of the great dinosaurs in bulk. But whatever the Loch Ness monster is, it has to be larger than the largest living reptile today. The great leathery or leather-backed turtle, which may reach an overall length of ten feet and is the largest of the living turtles (and one of the rarest), occasionally is seen in waters that are normally believed to be too cold for a reptile. This turtle, by the way, has sometimes been mistaken for a sea serpent.

But—it seems there always must be a but in subjects like this—if our hypothetical large Loch Ness reptile would take an unusually long time to cool off in the cold waters of the loch, it would also have to take an unusually long time to warm up as well. Reptiles usually warm up by basking in the sun. This means the Loch Ness monster would have to spend many hours a day sunning itself. At certain seasons of the year there isn't enough sun at Loch Ness to warm a garden snake. Since the Loch Ness monster has been seen winter as well as summer, the creature could not hibernate like other reptiles of northern regions. Besides, any large creature that spends a lot of time basking in the sun would almost surely be more visible than the Loch Ness monster has proved to be.

Must we, therefore, still rule out the plesiosaurs and all other reptiles as candidates because of cold weather? Not necessarily. There is a great deal we do not know about the dinosaurs and the other reptiles of past ages. Perhaps they were able to control their internal temperatures by more than sheer size. Those reptiles, which evolved into mammals at some point, did develop temperature control mechanisms. Perhaps some of the great reptiles, the dinosaurs and huge marine reptiles like the plesiosaurs, had done the same. We have no way of knowing, for all we have today are fossilized bones of the creatures. Bones cannot give us a complete story of the way they lived. The plesiosaurs, the dinosaurs, and the rest presumably died out seventy million years ago. So if you are extremely partial to the plesiosaur theory as an explanation for the Loch Ness monster there is still a slender thread of hope that Nessie may ultimately turn out to be some sort of huge primordial reptile.

In the mid 1960s the unique idea that Nessie was an invertebrate, a boneless giant, gained supporters in the ranks of the monster buffs. Dr. Roy P. Mackal, a microbiologist from the University of Chicago who had become thoroughly hooked on the Loch Ness search, proposed that Nessie was some sort of giant mollusc, probably a giant sea slug. Because of Mackal's scientific credentials the sea slug theory got a great deal of publicity in the press. Few scientists are willing to speculate publicly about the Loch Ness, or any other monster. They don't believe in them, are not interested, or do not want to get involved for fear of damaging their reputations.

Mackal's theory was, and is, ingenious because it accounts for many of the apparent paradoxical qualities attributed to the Loch Ness monster. But first we must ask if such a thing as a giant sea slug is possible. Most of us are familiar with the common garden slug, which looks like a snail without a shell. Marine varieties of the slug are quite common in the seas of the world and come in a great variety of exotic shapes and colors. But no known sea slug measures over a foot in length, and most of them are much smaller. But the sea slug is a mollusc, and so is the squid. As monster buffs never tire of pointing out, scientists did not believe there could be such a thing as a giant squid. The creatures were sighted time and again, and these sightings were brushed aside as hallucinations or tall tales. Only when the remains of giant squids were washed ashore was science belatedly forced to recognize that such creatures existed. A few unorthodox enthusiasts had proclaimed the existence of the giant squid all along. It is with these prophets that the monster buffs of today identify, and in whose footsteps they hope to follow. The giant squid is the largest known invertebrate. It may measure seventy feet or more (much more) from tip of tail to tip of tentacle. Therefore, theoretically at least, a sea slug of thirty or more feet is not biologically impossible.

Another problem is that all known sea slugs are just that— sea creatures, not inhabitants of lakes or other bodies of fresh water. Mackal saw no problem in countering this objection. Some five to seven thousand years ago Loch Ness was directly connected with the sea. Geological changes caused the land to rise, isolating the loch, which is now fifty-five feet above sea level. This change, Mackal's theory runs, trapped a small colony of giant sea slugs in the loch. As the water gradually changed from salt to fresh the creatures adapted, and they have been living there quietly ever since. Numerous examples of salt-water creatures adapting to fresh-water conditions can be found.

The really nice thing about the theoretical giant sea slug is that it can have a soft, squishy body. This might explain the problem of the bewilderingly variable number of humps that have been attributed to Nessie. Observers have reported anywhere from one to seven humps on the creature. No back-boned animal could have such variable back geometry. But a spineless sea slug just might.

A sea slug would be a shy, hard-to-find creature, which would explain why Nessie is not seen more often. The creature would breathe through gills and thus not have to come to the surface. Its above-the-water appearances would be rare, probably accidental, as seems to be the case with Nessie. Invertebrates are not notably inquisitive and would probably stay away from places where men were likely to be. They would not have the need or, for that matter, the ability to climb out onto dry land. The few sightings of Nessie out of the water could be explained in other ways.

A marked peculiarity of Loch Ness monster sightings is that the creature is seen far more frequently on calm days than on windy ones. This tendency is so marked that experienced monster watchers rarely bother to observe the loch on choppy days. If Nessie were a giant sea slug, then she presumably would have to keep her skin moist. Therefore, she would most carefully avoid the surface on windy days, for the wind would have a drying effect on the skin.

When the RAF experts examined the Dinsdale film they were impressed by the speed at which the object in it seemed to be moving. Many persons who have sighted what they believed to be the Loch Ness monster have mentioned the tremendous wave or wash the creature generated when it moved. Squids move by sucking in water and then expelling it with great force, a sort of underwater jet propulsion. If the hypothetical giant sea slug moved the same way, this could account for both the speed and the wash.

A dead sea slug would sink to the bottom and decay completely, leaving behind no telltale bones to betray its presence to the outside world.

While most of those who think they have seen the Loch Ness monster report only a hump or a series of them, a few others mention head and neck sightings. Then there is the famous London surgeon's photograph. Could a sea slug have a serpentine neck and small head? None of the known sea slugs do, but as we have pointed out the sea slugs are a remarkably varied tribe, so why not? A couple of sightings contain the mention of small projections like horns near the head. Most snails and garden slugs have distinct heads plus little hornlike projections.

Then we must ask whether people have really seen the head and neck of the creature. Most sightings report no eyes, mouth, or other distinctive features (except the occasional horns). The London surgeon's photograph shows no features. Could this "head and neck" really be something else—an air tube as possessed by some snails, or even a tentacle like that of the squids? The tentacle of a giant squid projecting above the water has on more than one occasion been mistaken for the head and neck of the Great Sea Serpent.

Food is the one place where the giant sea slug theory runs into serious problems. Slugs, land and sea, are vegetarians, as many a distressed gardner knows. There simply does not seem to be enough edible vegetable matter in Loch Ness to support a huge slug, much less a colony of them. Could the slugs have adapted to eating fish, which abound in the loch? The adaptation problem is more formidable than that of adapting from salt to fresh water, but still is it possible?

Another supporter of the "boneless giant" theory is F. W. (Ted) Holiday, writer, world traveler, and passionately dedicated monster watcher. Holiday thinks Nessie is some sort of gigantic worm, related perhaps to the marine bristle worm. He developed this theory at length in the book *The Great Orm of Loch Ness*. Holiday, like most serious Loch Ness investigators, deplores the word "monster." "It was an unfortunate choice of phrase since it tended to prejudice zoologists against the subject from the outset . . . I prefer the term Great Orm which derives from the Scandinavian *Sjö-orm* [sea-serpent]."

In 1962 Holiday spotted his "Great Orm" at the loch. "Just below the surface, I then made out a shape. It was thick in the middle and tapered towards the extremities. It was a sort of blackish-grey in colour . . . Its size . . . was between 40 and 45 feet."

From then on Holiday collected tape recordings of other people's sightings, old records, photographs, drawings, legends, and anything else that might relate to the Loch Ness monster. When Roy Mackal came to Loch Ness from the University of Chicago, he showed Holiday a photograph which was like a revelation to him. It was a photo of a model of the "Tully monster," a curious and fairly common little creature that lived in what is now Chicago some 280 million years ago. At that time the Chicago area was covered with water and it was in this shallow sea that the Tully monster swam.

Dr. E. S. Richardson, Jr., one of the first scientists to examine a fossil of the Tully monster, described his first encounter with it thus:

"Extraordinary it was, indeed, although not unnatural. Clearly outlined on the freshly exposed surface of a split concentration was the impression of a most curious prodigy. At one end of a dirigible-like body was a spade-shaped tail; from the other end extended a long thin proboscis with a gaping claw; across the body near the base of the proboscis was a transverse bar with a little round swelling at each end, outside the body."

The fossil had been brought to the Chicago Natural History Museum by Francis J. Tully, hence the creature's first name. Tully wanted the scientists to identify it, but they couldn't, so they started calling it the Tully monster. Although the little creature has gained a Latin scientific name, *Tullimonstrum gregarium* (*gregarium* means common), it still has not been fitted into any of the recognized zoological classifications.

The Tully monster model reminded Holiday of what he

had seen in the loch and it seemed to fit the other descriptions he had collected. He theorized that this ancient creature may have been a tiny ancestor of today's Nessie.

But today Holiday holds a minority opinion, for popular favor has swung away from the boneless giants and toward the mammals. The first explanations for Loch Ness monster sightings back in the 1930s were that the creature might be a seal or small whale that had somehow or other gotten into the loch. Such speculation was quickly submerged by the prehistoric reptile theory.

In the early 1960s Dr. Maurice Burton, a British naturalist who had once believed in the existence of the Loch Ness monster, finally came to the conclusion that there was no such animal. He did, however, admit that some of the sightings were puzzling and that they might have been caused by an unknown variety of long-necked otter—a mammal.

Since Burton was regarded as a renegade by the monster buffs (and thus worse than an ordinary nonbeliever) his otter suggestion was completely ignored. But then in 1968 Bernard Heuvelmans published his massive *In the Wake of Sea Serpents* where he concluded that he sea serpent (or monster) stories really resulted principally from the sightings of large and as yet unidentified kinds of aquatic mammals, including a theoretical "super otter."

At this writing Heuvelmans is at work on a companion volume to his sea monster study—this one to consider lake monsters. But he currently favors the mammal theory to explain the Loch Ness monster. There is no doubt that it is more exciting and satisfying to believe that Nessie is a giant mammal rather than a gigantic slug or worm. Heuvelmans himself identifies the Loch Ness monster with his own hypothetical "long-necked sea serpent." With Heuvelmans' prestige behind this identification, opinion has swung heavily toward the mammal theory. Even Roy Mackal, who con-

structed the very convincing giant sea slug theory, has gone
over to mammals, at least tentatively.

Mackal has now proposed that the Loch Ness monster is
a sirenian—one of a small order of mammals that includes
the manatees and dugong. Sirenians grow pretty large. In
1753 the German naturalist G. W. Steller discovered a huge
variety of sirenian living off the coast of a remote island in
the Bering Strait, between Siberia and Alaska. Steller's sea
cow, as the creature was named, grew to a length of thirty
feet. Within half a century after its discovery, however, this
peaceable sea giant was hunted out of existence by fishermen
and trappers who came to the northern seas in search of fish
and furs. (There was a report that a herd of creatures believed to be Steller's sea cows had been sighted by a Soviet
expedition in the Bering Strait in 1962, but the identification
was uncertain and no more has been heard of them. Most
zoologists conclude that the creature is extinct and has been
for a long time, for so large and visible an animal could not
have escaped detection.)

Despite the popular impression that the Loch Ness monster is fifty or one hundred feet long, a creature of thirty feet
or less could easily account for the vast majority of sightings.
So this hypothetical Loch Ness sirenian would not have to be
any larger than Steller's sea cow. But aquatic mammals are
usually compact in shape, and the sirenians have virtually no
neck, while the Loch Ness reports indicate a creature with a
very long neck. So if the thing in the loch is a serenian it
would have had to undergo a considerable modification in
structure.

A sirenian would also have had to undergo another important modification. Steller's sea cow and all other sirenians
are vegetarians. But, as mentioned, there is precious little
edible vegetable matter in the loch. Nessie almost has to be
a fish eater. But again, the adaptation is not outside the realm

of biological possibility. One more adaptation—an easy one—would have to be from salt water to fresh. Sirenians are all sea creatures but many other aquatic mammals, some dolphins and seals, for example, have made this transition.

Steller's sea cow provides us with an interesting explanation for the puzzling "humps" of the monster. The creature's scientific name is *Rhytina stelleri,* literally Steller's wrinkled one. The creature's body was encased in great rolls or folds of fat. Such rolls just sticking above the surface might look like the series of humps so often described. But other explanations for the humps are also possible. Sirenians, like all other aquatic mammals, swim with an up-and-down motion, while most fish swim with a side-to-side motion. Up-and-down motion could give the appearance of humps in the water. Mackal believes that the humps can be accounted for by two or more of the sociable monsters basking near the surface together. It might even be caused by a young monster riding on its mother's back, a behavior pattern well known among sirenians.

But wouldn't an air-breathing mammal have to come to the surface more often than the Loch Ness monster does? Not at all, say the monster watchers. Of all aquatic mammals, sirenians are particularly shy, secretive creatures. They can stay under water a half hour at a time and when they do come up to breathe they may do so merely by sticking the tips of their nostrils above the surface. Such surfacing would hardly be noticeable.

Sirenians and other aquatic mammals are known for their particularly acute sense of hearing, and many reports indicate Nessie's extreme sensitivity to noise. Clem Skelton tells of how slamming a car door on the shore caused the monster, who was basking more than fifty feet away, to sink out of sight at once.

Unlike seals, and sea lions, sirenians are never known to

leave the water voluntarily. There is some evidence that Steller's sea cow was able to do so under the press of necessity. This would account for the Loch Ness monster's infrequent jaunts onto the land.

By matching sirenian characteristics with the reported characteristics of the Loch Ness monster, one may build a fairly impressive case—on paper. The chief objection is that it seems extremely unlikely that any large mammal could live as unobtrusively in Loch Ness as the monster seems able to. True enough, aquatic mammals differ a great deal in "visibility." Sea lions are gregarious and obvious. Most living sirenians avoid detection whenever possible. But the great northern sea cow discovered by Steller was not a hard-to-find animal. It was so obvious that it was quickly and easily hunted to extinction. Even the secretive North American manatee quickly betrays its presence to a trained observer.

Unlike a worm or slug, the hypothetical sirenian would leave behind bones when it died. Mackal has suggested dredging the bottom of Loch Ness for remains of the monster, but so far no extensive dredging operations have been undertaken. Would any of these bones or a carcass itself ever have been washed ashore? The sides of the loch are quite steep in most places, and not much of anything gets washed ashore. Still, the total absence of any remains, although not conclusive, is disturbing. Disturbing too is the absence of footprints (or in this case flipper prints) left behind by the creature during its occasional land sojourns.

Monster buffs are fond of saying that objections like those raised above are merely "negative evidence," and thus do not really count for much when stacked up against the "positive evidence" of sightings and pictures. None of these objections destroy the case for the Loch Ness monster beyond repair, but they do raise the odds against it.

A fish, most probably a giant eel, has occasionally been

advanced as a candidate for the Loch Ness monster. But this hypothesis has never gained many supporters. One suspects that the reason is that it is just not exotic enough. If the fabled monster turned out to be nothing more than a big fish, even a fish previously unknown to science, it would be rather disappointing. There are also realistic objections to this theory. Fish do not swim around with their heads and necks out of water—in fact, fish do not even have necks. No known fish has ever remotely resembled the plesiosaur-like description that has most commonly been attributed to Nessie.

One of the major objections to the existence of the Loch Ness monster is that if it ever lived it should surely be extinct by now. Monster buffs speak of a breeding herd of monsters in the loch. But because of the rarity of the sightings and the limited size of the loch that herd would, of necessity, be extremely small. With animals, when the numbers of an individual species fall low enough, extinction becomes inevitable in the long run. Yet we are asked to accept that this small and isolated herd has been able to maintain a stable population for thousands of years.

Most monster buffs somehow connect the Loch Ness monster with the Great Sea Serpent. If the creatures in the loch could be replenished from the vast sea, then the extinction objection would no longer be valid. I once thought I had devised a way round this problem, a way in which Loch Ness monsters could get from the loch to the sea or vice versa. Loch Ness is connected with the sea, miles away, by the River Ness. The river is quite shallow and runs right through the middle of the city of Inverness. The thought of a large and strange creature paddling its way, unnoticed, through the middle of Inverness is absurd. So the migration of the Loch Ness monster, as an adult, from the sea to the loch must be discounted. But what if the creature conducted this migration when it was at a stage of life when it was neither large nor unusual-looking. For the moment this seemed an inspiration.

Newly hatched eels, or elvers, are only a tiny fraction of the size of a fully grown eel. Moreover, they do not resemble the adult. The difference is so striking that for many years scientists were unable to relate the two stages. They were thought to be a different species. No one could figure out where the baby eels went. Unlike salmon many eels are hatched in the sea, return to fresh water where they grow to maturity, then return once again to the sea to spawn.

What does this have to do with the Loch Ness Monster? If there were an eel—a giant one perhaps—that bred in the sea then swam to fresh water to mature? (The larva of what may be a giant eel has been found.) The relatively tiny larva of this hypothetical eel might pass up the River Ness unnoticed. Once in the loch they would grow into the giant that is known as the Loch Ness monster. Since eels often migrate vast distances to reach a particular spot, this giant eel might be peculiar to Loch Ness and perhaps a couple of other lakes where similar creatures have been reported.

For about a half hour I thought I had found the key to this most vexing aspect of the Loch Ness problem. Then I began to wonder how the adult eels got back into the sea to breed again. Of course, they couldn't get out unnoticed as adults, any more than they could get in unnoticed. Indeed, a giant eel could not get out at all, for the river is simply too shallow.

I contrived various ingenious ways of saving my theory. First, I postulated alternating life cycles. One generation, bred in salt water, migrated to the loch and matured. That generation then bred in the fresh water of Loch Ness and migrated out of the loch as immature specimens and back into the ocean. Far stranger life cycles are known in nature, but still that seemed to be reaching.

Another possibility I came up with was that Loch Ness

was a sort of giant eels' graveyard—a dead end for those who mistakenly swim into it. Thousands of years ago, when Loch Ness was an arm of the sea my hypothetical giant eel habitually migrated there. As the land rose and Loch Ness became isolated from the ocean the elvers continued their old habits, for such migration patterns seem imprinted on the very biological makeup of many animals. Very clever. That theory would work for a single generation only. After one generation had migrated into the loch, become trapped, and died out, that would be that. No future giant eels would ever get a chance to develop that particular migration pattern.

These speculations are no more farfetched than many that have been advanced quite seriously. I recount them to show what one can do with a little biological knowledge and a little imagination. We must conclude, and most monster buffs would agree, that if there really is any large and strange creature in Loch Ness it is born, lives out its life, and dies there. This leaves the extinction problem as the most formidable obstacle to belief in the Loch Ness monster.

Yet another obstacle in the way of belief concerns the creature's food. If the Loch Ness monster eats fish, as is commonly supposed, then it must be an astonishingly efficient fish catcher. Most large fish eaters miss much of their prey. Often they leave wounds—telltale scars—on their intended victims. Although Loch Ness is not as heavily fished as it once was, there are still many fish taken out of the loch. No fisherman has ever encountered fish bearing wounds that seem as though they might have been inflicted by a large unknown animal.

All in all, the Loch Ness monster seems a most improbable beast. Then, there are many improbable creatures in nature. However, in order to accept the improbable, evidence for its existence has to be fairly strong. "I don't see how anyone who has examined all the evidence can come to any conclusion other than that there is a large and unknown creature living in Loch Ness," says Clem Skelton. His view is echoed by virtually everyone closely connected with the monster search. Over the years a few former enthusiasts like Maurice Burton have fallen away from true belief and despaired of ever finding anything unknown in the loch, but the majority have remained remarkably faithful and enthusiastic. Each year the search continues a little something new seems to be added to the dossier in the case for the monster.

Even a hardened skeptic must treat the case for the Loch Ness monster with some respect. Unfortunately, there is not an ounce of physical evidence, not a bone, not a scale, or even a footprint. A joker who made tracks around the loch with a stuffed hippopotamus foot created a minor sensation some years ago, but the hoax was quickly exposed. A strange bone reportedly found by the loch in 1969 turned out to be the jawbone of a small whale that had once decorated a museum curator's rock garden.

On the positive side, there are the sonar readings, disputed but not entirely discredited, the Dinsdale film, and some other long-distance motion pictures which show no detail but are at least intriguing. Then there are several still photos. Many of these were unfortunately taken at such a distance that they show no detail. Others, including a couple of really remarkable ones, are generally considered to be hoaxes, even by the buffs. But there are two quite good photos which must be discussed.

First there is "the famous London surgeon's photograph," taken in 1934. The surgeon himself, Kenneth Wilson, remained maddeningly obscure about what he saw when he took the picture. The photo itself shows what appears to be the snakelike neck and head of the Loch Ness monster sticking above the water. The great problem with the picture is that it shows only the object and the water. There are no shore objects against which one can make a size comparison, or indeed determine if the photo actually was taken at Loch Ness. Using such factors as the angle of the camera and the lens focal length, various experts have decided that the object could be anywhere from two to eight feet out of the water. The difference is vital. If it is only two feet, then the photo's value as evidence is severely reduced, because then the photo might be of the tail of a diving otter, rather than the head of an emerging monster. Maurice Burton examined many photos of otters going down and found that some of them do bend the tips of their tails in a way which closely approximates the object shown in the surgeon's photograph. The surgeon said that he photographed what appeared to be an eight-foot object two or three hundred yards away. Burton countered that he had really photographed a two-foot object a mere twenty-five feet away. Could such a mistake be made honestly? Yes, answered Burton, the surgeon was misled because the sun was in his eyes and distances over water are extremely difficult to judge. There the surgeon's photo controversy rests for the present.

In 1955, P. A. MacNab photographed what he took to be the monster. The photo shows two humps, one looking like an upturned boat, and the other looking like a somewhat smaller upturned boat. No other features are visible, and the photo would not be worth much except it was taken near the ruins of Urquhart Castle, a picturesquely crumbling ruin on the loch. The castle's tower shows clearly in the photo. From the known size of the tower some estimate of the size of the monster can be made. If the humps belong to a single creature, it could be over fifty feet in length. If they are two creatures swimming near one another, the larger could be thirty feet long. Less impressive than the surgeon's photo and less well publicized than the Dinsdale films, this photo is considered by many monster buffs to be the best piece of tangible evidence in the monster's dossier.

Basically, however, the case for the Loch Ness monster rests on the thousands of sightings that have been reported since the early 1930s. Even if one discounts mistakes and possible hoaxes—knocking out eighty to ninety percent of the reports as the Loch Ness Phenomena Investigation Bureau does—the number of acceptable reports is impressive.

When talking to some of the people who have made sightings, one is almost overwhelmed by their apparent sincerity and good sense. "I couldn't be fooled," says old Alex Campbell looking you straight in the eye, "not for a moment." But not everyone who lives near Loch Ness has seen the monster or believes in it. Nor are all the locals even interested in the creature. The real enthusiasts are outsiders—Englishmen and Americans. The locals regard the monster buffs as curiosities at least as strange as anything that might be living in the loch. "They think we're all a bit potty," one of the buffs said, and then after a moment's reflection added, "Perhaps we are."

Enthusiasm for the Loch Ness monster will wax and wane, but the search in one form or another will continue until The Picture is taken, or some other piece of conclusive and incontrovertible evidence is found, or until the loch is drained dry and shown to contain nothing larger than a salmon.

While the Loch Ness monster captured much of the attention that had once been focused on the Great Sea Serpent, ripples from Nessie's wake have also awakened interest in other large unknown creatures that are supposed to dwell in the depths of fresh-water lakes. Using the celebrated Loch Ness monster as a news peg, the press began reporting lake-monster stories from many parts of the globe. Members of the Loch Ness Phenomena Investigation Bureau and a number of individual monster buffs started collecting press clippings and other reports of such creatures. Soon the list of possible lake monsters was staggering. It seems as though every large lake and a goodly number of small ones as well have a monster of their own. Evidence for the existence of these numerous monsters, or even authentic tradition concerning them, represents rather a mixed bag. Often the evidence is no more than a single newspaper clipping reporting a single sighting—the witnesses may be unnamed, or turn out to be a group of teen-agers or children. Tradition may be no more than some old fellow who says he saw it or heard about it back around the turn of the century. But there are a considerable number of cases where the sightings are not so easily brushed aside as hoax or delusion.

Interest first centered on those bodies of water closest to Loch Ness itself, the other lochs of the Highlands of Scotland. Tim Dinsdale in his book *The Leviathans* lists multiple monster sightings in Lochs Oich, Lochy, Linnhe, Eil, Arkaig, Shiel, Morar, and Quoich. All of these lochs form part of, or are near, the Great Glen.

Oddly, Dinsdale lists no reports from Loch Treig, a near neighbor of Loch Ness, which, in the opinion of Dr. A. Stewart, once boasted "the largest, wildest, fiercest breed of waterbulls in the world."

Even famed Loch Lomond to the south has had its monster sightings. In 1964 a butcher and his wife saw what they took to be a monster's hump in the loch. But the buffs have difficulty accepting tales of the Loch Lomond monster. The same difficulties will arise again in regard to other lake monsters. Loch Lomond is huge; it actually covers a greater area than Loch Ness, although it is not as deep. In the eighteenth century, Loch Lomond was still wild enough to allow the famous outlaw Rob Roy to have his hideout on its shores. But today Loch Lomond, an easy drive from Glasgow, Scotland's largest city, is a popular vacation spot. Every summer thousands of Scots brave its chilly waters to go swimming. Boating on the Loch is an increasingly popular sport. Loch Ness is still relatively remote, but it is almost impossible to believe that so well used a body of water as Loch Lomond could contain any large unknown animal.

In 1969 Loch Morar became the focus of monster interest. Loch Morar is a good place for a monster because it is 1017 feet deep, making it even deeper than Loch Ness (although it is not nearly as large in total area). Late in the summer, two Sunday fishermen, William Simpson and Duncan McDonnell, said they were rowing across the loch when a monster popped up next to their boat. It was described as being about sixty feet long, dark brown in color, and having several round humps. McDonnell tried to chase it away with an oar from the boat, but the monster bit the end off the oar. Simpson took more drastic action by firing at the creature with a shotgun. He said the blast dug a four-inch hole in the thing and "it dived below the surface." No one has seen Morag—as the monster of Loch Morar has been dubbed—since the shooting.

The Irish, of course, are not deficient either in legends of fresh-water monsters or in modern sightings. In going through a book called *Irish Names of Places,* a turn-of-the-century account of Irish traditions and folklore, Dinsdale ran across a paragraph which links the Loch Ness monster to some of the Irish lake monsters.

"Legends of aquatic monsters are very ancient among the Irish people. We find one mentioned by Adamnan as infesting Loch Ness in Scotland. In the life of St. Mochua of Balla, it is related that a stag which was wounded in the chase took refuge on an island in Lough Ree; but that no one dared to follow it on account of a horrible Monster that infested the lake, and was accustomed to destroy swimmers. A man was at last prevailed to swim across, 'but as he was returning the beast devoured him.' "

The significance of this account is that *Irish Names of Places* was written well before the current Loch Ness "flap" began in the 1930s. The legend of the Loch Ness monster must have been well known enough to be related to similar legends in Ireland. Adamnan's original story of the man-eating monster of Loch Ness sounds so much like the story of the man-eating monster of Lough Ree that it is possible to conclude the Irish simply copied it, or that both stories are drawn from the same ancient Celtic tradition of man-eating lake monsters.

Some of the Irish lakes which have a good tradition of water monsters plus a good record of modern sightings would seem to be admirable places for investigation. These lakes are more accessible and smaller than Loch Ness. The waters are clearer and warmer, thus affording divers an excellent opportunity for underwater observation and photography.

I asked some members of the Loch Ness Phenomena Investigation Bureau why they did not concentrate at least a part of their efforts on these easily studied lakes, rather than spending all their time at deep, dark, and difficult Loch Ness. Although they were quite firm in their belief that monsters live in bodies of fresh water other than Loch Ness, they were also quite candid about their fears concerning the "easy" Irish lakes. "What happens if the monster turns out to be just a big snapping turtle, or nothing at all?" one of them asked me. "We would be a laughingstock. Everyone would say that just because that lake didn't have a monster then Loch Ness didn't either."

The Scandinavian countries, home of the earliest sea serpent reports, are also the home of some of the best lake-monster reports. Perhaps the most well-authenticated reports come from a lake called Storsjön in central Sweden. This lake is located at 63°N latitude, which is pretty far north and means that the lake is frozen for several months of the year. Storsjön covers 176 square miles. In the local museum in the town of Ostersund on the lake's east shore are some enormous spring traps which, according to the local residents, were used at the end of the last century in an attempt to catch the monster of the lake. The curator of this museum wrote Tim Dinsdale that the "Great Lake Monster" seemed most active from 1820 to 1898, when it was seen twenty-two times, "mostly by trustworthy persons." Although it had been seen less frequently in the twentieth century, the monster had by no means disappeared entirely.

This particular monster has been described in more detail than the Loch Ness monster. Writes the curator: "The head is said to be round and smooth like that of a dog, with great eyes . . . the extremities are described as short, stumpy legs or feet, possibly big clumsy fins, possibly long, webbed hind legs. It has great fins on the back of the head, possibly ears, described as little sails, which can be laid tight on the neck."

In general, however, with its elongated shape, humps, and fondness for basking on the surface in fine, calm weather, the Great Lake Monster of Sweden resembles its counterpart in Loch Ness.

The wildest of the modern lake-monster stories have come out of the vast expanses of the eastern part of the Soviet Union. Although the stories concern a dozen different lakes most have a distinct similarity. A group of scientists or explorers come upon a remote lake. The simple villages in the vicinity warn them of the monster in the lake, but they don't believe what these simple folk say until they are confronted by the horrible creature.

It is difficult to know what to make of these stories. Either the lakes of the eastern Soviet Union have an extraordinarily large supply of highly visible monsters or Soviet scientists and explorers are very vulnerable to hoax and hallucination.

There is a third alternative. Stories from the Soviet Union particularly from remote areas are notoriously difficult to check out. As a result, both fraud and error can get a pretty wide circulation before the source of the story is run down, if it ever is. It is significant to note that none of these monster stories ever seems to have a follow-up. The monster is never captured or photographed, or even discussed at international scientific meetings in which Soviet scientists participate.

In the early 1960s there were repeated stories that Soviet radio astronomers had been picking up intelligent signals from outer space. As it turned out, Soviet astronomers had been picking up signals from space which they could not explain. One of the younger and more daring scientists had speculated on the possibility that these signals might have an intelligent origin. As it turned out, they didn't. But the press, Soviet and Western, had inflated this speculation into "fact."

Stories of the discovery of a prehistoric monster swimming around Lake Baikal were based on "an authentic and accurately reported Soviet source," but the source was a science fiction story. How and why this fiction was passed off as fact in the Western press is not clear.

Over the years I have worked as a science writer, I have heard so many rumors of flying saucer studies, sensational ESP research, secret satellite launchings, and the like in the Soviet Union that I have become quite frankly suspicious of any bizarre story supposed to have originated there. So many individuals engaged in offbeat "research," be they monster buffs or flying saucer addicts, claim to have a "scientist" or group of "scientists" in Russia feeding them these wild stories that one simply has to sit back and wait for more tangible proof to appear. It never seems to.

Of the many Soviet lake monsters, that of Lake Khaiyr, a lake deep in the tundra of Siberia, has been described most fully. A biologist named N. F. Gladkikh reportedly almost fell over the thing one morning. Whatever it was had climbed out of the water and was eating the grass on the shore of the lake. It had a small head on a long shiny neck, an enormous body with bluish-black skin, and an upright dorsal fin. By the time Gladkikh brought the other members of his party to the lake the thing was gone, but they did see trampled grass and observe strange ripples in the water. Jokers have dubbed this creature the "Lochski Nesski Monsterovich."

Lake Victoria in Central Africa is the second largest freshwater lake in the world. It is some two hundred fifty miles long and two hundred miles wide and, quite naturally, it too contains a monster. In fact, there are two distinct monster traditions attached to Victoria. The first concerns a fearful roaring serpent that rises out of the lake and swallows up everything in its path. Joy of joys, this is one legend that with fair certainty can be traced back to its source. Lake Victoria is susceptible to waterspouts—aquatic tornadoes in which a column of water is sucked up and whirled about at great speed. Descriptions of the roaring serpent leave little doubt that it is really a waterspout.

The second lake monster in Victoria is the *lukwata*. The native accounts of the beast are sketchy. From them one writer concluded that the creature "might either be a small cetacean [whale] or a large form of manatee or, more probably, a gigantic fish." The one European who reported seeing the *lukwata* of Lake Victoria got only a brief glimpse, and described it as having a roundish shape and dark color. This is not a very helpful description.

There seems to be no current tradition concerning large unknown animals in Lake Victoria. Besides, that lake is really a poor place for a monster. Victoria is very large, but not very deep—its greatest known depth being a mere two hundred seventy feet. Loch Ness, you will recall, is over seven hundred feet deep. A really large animal would have had difficulty remaining hidden in less than three hundred feet of water.

Next to Loch Ness itself the best of the fresh-water monster reports come, surprisingly enough, from Canada. They originate at Lake Okanagan, a long narrow lake (seventy-five miles long, three and a half miles wide at its widest point) in British Columbia. The monster of Lake Okanagan is called Ogopogo, and as you might guess it got its name from an Indian legend about a monster in the lake.

The summer population of boaters and tourists at Lake Okanagan is considerable, and in recent years the vacationers have not seen too much of Ogopogo. As is typical with lake monsters, most of the sightings are made on fine sunny days. But now, on such a day, the lake is crisscrossed by motorboats. These noisy boats, in the opinion of the buffs, have kept Ogopogo underwater and out of sight.

Still, there have been enough reports to convince some of the locals and the world-wide monster-watching community of the reality of Ogopogo. *The New York Times* once offered one thousand dollars for a good picture of the beast, but the prize was never collected.

According to a locally produced booklet on the subject: "Descriptions vary . . . but broadly follow the same general pattern. The length is placed from thirty to seventy feet . . . The infrequent descriptions of the head agree that it has the general appearance of a sheep. Some claim there were whiskers or a beard. Almost all observers report that the body was coiled or humped, the tops of the humps showing plainly above the lake's surface. All agree too that he can move very rapidly . . ."

Lake Okanagan is well suited for investigation. It is narrow enough to be kept under observation by a relatively small team of land-based observers. It is not in a remote place, so investigators would not have to endure either great hardship or great expense getting there. And yet the investigation of Ogopogo has remained a rather casual and haphazard affair. Perhaps it will not always remain so. Writes Dinsdale, "Unless I am mistaken, the Ogopogo will in due time become a focal point of interest, and Okanagan Lake subject to the most intense scientific probing."

The name Ogopogo is infectious. A monster that has been reported in Lake Winnipegosis, Manitoba, has been dubbed Manipogo. The Manipogo reports, unfortunately, are not very impressive, although they were good enough to stimulate one University of Manitoba professor to go out and hunt for the "thing."

Manipogo does have one distinction. It is the only lake monster that is reported to have left behind definite physical proof of its reality. In the 1930s a local man named Oscar Fredrickson was supposed to have found a huge vertebra in the lake. Sadly, at some point between that day and this, the original vertebra was destroyed in a fire. But a wooden replica of the original bone remains.

It is hard to be hopeful about Manipogo on the basis of such flimsy evidence. Lake Winnipegosis itself is quite shallow and not at all the sort of place in which a monster could successfully hide.

If the evidence for Manipogo is flimsy, the evidence for Igopogo is so thin that even the enthusiasts are openly cautious. (The name is a pretty good clue as to how seriously we should take this one.) This creature is supposed to dwell in Lake Simcoe, Ontario. The problem is that the lake is a bare forty miles from Toronto, and is an extremely popular summer resort. The appearance of a monster among the bathers and boaters of Lake Simcoe should create more of an impression than it has. Evidence for the existence of this creature is little more than a handful of newspaper clippings.

This by no means exhausts the list of possible fresh-water monsters. Reports concerning a dozen or so lakes in the continental United States and an equal number in South America have been collected.

What are we dealing with here? A world-wide epidemic of huge and unknown fresh-water creatures? Hardly. The idea that a large unknown animal could exist in a shallow well-explored lake strains our credulity.

Even in the best of the cases, like those of Loch Ness and Lake Okanagan, the evidence is disconcertingly flabby. We can't easily dismiss either Nessie or Ogopogo as a joke, but reservations—very strong reservations—must be expressed regarding a belief in their reality.

If the widespread belief in lake monsters is not based on the sightings of real monsters, what is it based on? The most cynical explanation is that the monster flaps started as hoaxes cooked up by local hotel owners and encouraged by sensational journalists. No doubt there is some truth in this charge, but the influence of the conscious hoaxer has often been exaggerated.

At one time or another most people, from Highland Scots to American Indians, have believed in some sort of monster or powerful spirit that lived in deep lakes. Most of these "monsters" may have been merely the tangible embodiment of the dangers poised to men by the unknown waters. We often people the dangerous unknown with monstrous shapes and forms.

Today, however, the dangerous unknown on the earth has shrunk almost to the vanishing point. We are beginning to miss it. Without it a good deal of the flavor and excitement has gone out of life. So we grasp at every hint that there is really something large and strange lurking out there beneath the surface.

The lake-monster myths that we build for ourselves today

are quite different from those that were woven by people of past ages. In the Dark Ages the Loch Ness monster was a fierce beast who gobbled up swimmers and could be put to flight only by the intervention of an authentic saint. Today the poor monster is so timid that he barely ever shows himself.

The people of the Dark Ages who lived near Loch Ness probably believed implicitly in the monster, and they would have been vastly relieved to discover that no monster really existed. Today, while there are many people who do not believe that the Loch Ness monster exists, there is practically no one who would not be overjoyed to find out that it did.

The Hairy Wild Ones

Despite the popularity of skin diving we are not really water animals. For most of us, seas and lakes remain mysterious and a bit frightening. As we have seen, even in the twentieth century they are populated by a great variety of monsters, real or imaginary. But the number of land monsters has decreased sharply in modern times. They have either been recognized and classified by zoologists (thus immediately losing their monster status) or they have proved to be like the chimera—chimerical.

Stories of this or that large curious beast do filter out of jungles and swamps in distant parts of the world—they may rate a newspaper article or even a longer article in one of the more sensational men's magazines—but belief is feeble. Today there is only one land monster which has a large following. This monster is big, covered with hair, vaguely human, often dangerous, and usually a resident of mountainous areas. It has been known under a bewildering variety of names. Unfortunately, the most familiar name is also the worst—the Abominable Snowman.

Abominable Snowman is really an abominable name. It is cumbersome, confusing, inaccurate, and in the view of some of the creature's friends, downright insulting. They ask, with some justification, what right do we have to call anything "abominable"? But Abominable Snowman is the name that has captured the public attention, and we are stuck with it. The increasingly popular term Yeti is not an adequate substitute for Abominable Snowman. Yeti properly refers only to a creature of the Himilayas, and, as we shall see, this particular monsters is ubiquitous. Only a few are familar with the other names, like the Wild Man, *Meh-Teh*, Sasquatch, Bigfoot, Mountain Giant, and a score of other local names under which this creature, or variations of it, are known.

Everyone has heard something about the Abominable Snowman. Perhaps you have heard of the footprints reportedly seen and photographed by mountain climbers high in the Himalayan snow fields. Perhaps you have heard that the people of the mountains of Tibet, Nepal, Sikkim, and Bhutan are supposed to regard the creature as part of the local fauna. But this is only a portion of the total Abominable Snowman story. Indeed, this monster not only has an extraordinarily wide geographical spread—having been reported everywhere from Nepal to the state of Wisconsin—it also has one of the most extensive legendary histories of any modern monster.

Of course, way back in history the creature was not called the Abominable Snowman. We can identify him, whatever his name, by his characteristics. He is wild, hairy, very strong, inhabits mountainous or at least deserted places, and is nearly but not quite human.

He appears first in the oldest piece of literature still extant, the Gilgamesh Epic, which was probably set down by the

Sumerians. In this epic we find Enkidu, first the mortal enemy, and then firm friend of the hero Gilgamesh. Enkidu is a wild man covered with hair, who grew up in the desert among the beasts.

References in the Bible are not quite as clear, but they are there. When Saint Jerome translated the Bible from Hebrew to Latin, he translated a Hebrew word meaning demon to the Latin word *pilosi* which means "hairy one." The Prophet Isaiah described the deserted ruins of Babylon and in his translation Saint Jerome wrote, "and the hairy ones shall dance there." In another Isaiah prophecy of a scene of destruction Saint Jerome translates, "and one hairy creature will shout to the other." Exactly what Isaiah meant we do not know, but some scholars believe that the Hebrew demon was, as Jerome implied, a hairy creature who lived in deserted and ruined places.

Monster buffs make a good deal of the story of the twins Esau and Jacob described in Genesis. They were the sons of Isaac and Rebekah. The birth of Esau is described thus: "And the first came out red, all over like an hairy garment; and they called his name Esau" (Gen. 25:25). Later Jacob says, "Behold, Esau my brother is a hairy man, and I am a smooth man" (Gen. 27:11).

Of the two Esau was the wilder, "a cunning hunter," while Jacob "was a plain man, dwelling in tents."

Rebekah favored smooth Jacob, the second born of the twins, and connived to have him steal Esau's birthright. Isaac had grown old and his eyesight was very weak. He knew he was going to die, and wished to give his blessing to Esau, his eldest son and heir. But Rebekah wrapped Jacob's hands and neck in goatskins, to give them a properly hairy feel. She dressed him in Esau's robe, which had a singular and powerful odor. At least one commentator also believes the original Biblical text indicates that Jacob imitated Esau's voice by making deep growling sounds. In any case, Isaac was taken in, "and he discerned him not, because his hands were hairy, as his brother Esau's hands: so he blessed him" (Gen. 27:23).

From the Bible we next look for our hairy friends in classical mythology. Here the satyrs and fauns fall quite properly within our investigation. In the King James Version of the Bible, Isaiah's "demons" and Saint Jerome's "hairy ones" are translated as satyrs. The most memorable features of these creatures (aside from their enormous sexual appetites) were their little horns and goat feet—distinctly not Abominable Snowman characteristics. But they were hairy, or at least half-hairy, and most of the early representations show them as having monkey or apelike features. The satyrs were not exactly gods or spirits; that is, there was nothing supernatural about them. The early Greeks apparently believed that the satyrs were a real race or hairy, wild, manlike creatures that lived in forests and mountains.

The god Silenus was often to be found in the company of the fauns and satyrs. Later mythology was to soften the view of Silenus, converting him to a fat old man, very wise and very drunk. But the most ancient representations of Silenus show him as frighteningly ferocious, strong, and wild. He used an uprooted tree as a weapon. Painters and sculptors often gave Silenus a hairy body, as a sign of his wildness. When a Silenus character appeared in plays his costume was a shaggy garment.

Actually, Silenus did not originate with the Greeks. He seems to have been adopted from the sileni, an entire tribe of wild forest spirits that formed part of the mythology of the Phrygians of Asia Minor.

The Romans too had their shaggy wild god. He was Silvanius, a rather vaguely defined divinity, who seems to have had power over all those lands which lay beyond the fringes of cultivation. He was unpredictable and dangerous. Prudent Roman farmers habitually made some sort of offering to Silvanius before felling trees to make a new field or otherwise making inroads on this wild god's domain. Later, as the Romans became acquainted with the mythology of other peoples, Silvanius became thoroughly mixed in with the fauns, satyrs, and the sileni whom he in many ways resembled.

The Anglo-Saxon epic *Beowulf* contains a dandy Abominable Snowman-like character, the fiend Grendel. Grendel and his folk had been banished to the swamps and marshes by God. He is described as belonging with the ghouls, the dragons, the lemurs, the elves, the giants, and all the creatures that had been outlawed along with Satan. But Grendel is basically a wild man "drooling with spit, stinking and hairy." If there ever has been an abominable creature, Grendel is it.

The conquests of Alexander the Great opened up the "mysterious East" to Greek travelers and scholars. The stories of the wild inhabitants of these Eastern lands that filtered back to Europe were often quite fabulous. There were the forest people who had no mouths but had to subsist solely on the smell of roast meat and flowers. There were people with arms like snakes, or saws, and others who had no heads, but had faces in the middle of their chests.

Other tales, which may have sounded equally unbelievable in Europe, seem to have been substantially accurate. Pliny wrote about the Silverstres, a race of wild men in India who had hairy bodies, yellow eyes, long pointed teeth, and communicated by means of horrible shrieks. That is just the way the Indian gibbon would be described by someone who had never seen one before.

During the Middle Ages, all the stories of the wonders of the East—real and unreal—became incorporated into the "Alexander Romance." The romance is a cycle of legends and stories woven about the life of Alexander the Great. They are much like the legends that surrounded King Arthur, except that Alexander was a popular Persian as well as European hero. Since, like the legends of Arthur, the stories of the Alexander Romance were being continually rewritten and added to, it is virtually impossible to trace the source of any particular incident in them. What is important for our purposes is that these widly read and extremely influential stories were dotted with accounts of wild, hairy, manlike creatures that dwelt in the East, particularly in India. Perhaps only the uneducated took the Alexander Romance as literal truth, but even the scholars believed that the stories contained at least a "core of truth."

The fabulous races of the Alexander Romance were included in medieval encyclopedias. When some of the great travelers of the Middle Ages finally did visit the lands of the "mysterious East," they often confirmed the existence of totally mythical creatures.

Why, one wonders, did the European travelers declare that they had seen men with faces in their chests or men with hands and feet like saws? Were the travelers just plain liars? Some of them were—after all, there was no way the accuracy of their stories could easily be checked. For this reason the term "traveler's tale" means story of dubious merit. But many travelers were not liars, and probably reported what they thought was the truth.

The medieval European traveler in Asia did not have the advantage of a rent-a-car. His mobility was limited. If he wanted to find out about a particular creature, especially if this creature lived in a hard-to-reach place, he could not easily go and see for himself. So he might have to ask his host about the creature. Commonly, guest and host had only the barest understanding of one another's language, so both question and answer were in dire peril of being misunderstood.

Sometime the Oriental host might attest to the existence of a totally mythical creature, because he really believed it did exist—the creature being part of the mythology of his own land. Still other Eastern hosts seeing how earnestly their European guest desired to find out about a particular creature told him what they thought he wanted to hear, even though they knew it was untrue. This might have seemed the polite thing to do. Then it would be foolish for us to assume that the people of India or other Eastern lands were entirely without a sense of humor. They might have enjoyed fooling the foreigner.

So, for a variety of reasons, the first travelers tended to confirm rather than deny even the silliest of fables.

The evidence for the existence of a hairy, apelike, wild man in the East seemed overwhelming. Roger Bacon, one of the best educated men of thirteenth-century Europe, accepted the hairy wild man evidence without reservation. Bacon wrote that in the "high rocks" of Tibet and China (perhaps the mountains of Central Asia) there dwelt a hairy apelike creature. This is getting very close to the most popular homeland of the Abominable Snowman. But then Bacon adds a rather surprising and suspiciously familiar detail. The natives of Asia, Bacon says, capture this creature by getting it drunk. This recalls a Greek myth about how hairy old Silenus was captured by Greek shepherds after they got him drunk. Somehow, it seems Bacon is getting Greek mythology mixed in with his tales from the East.

One of the more intriguing wild man tales comes from the English adventurer Edward Webbe. In 1590 Webbe published what he said was an accurate account of his travels in the East. In the account he has a description of a hairy wild man that he saw chained to a post. This ferocious creature was fed the bodies of executed criminals, for it craved only human flesh. Webbe really did travel extensively in the East, but he said he saw the man-eating wild man at the court of Prester John, a Christian king of the East who, we now know, was a completely mythical character.

But we do not have to go out to India or back to the Babylonian epics and the Bible to find stories of this wild and hairy creature. From medieval times onward, Europe boasted a rich tradition of native lore concerning a hairy creature known simply as the wild man. Many of the wild man's attributes undoubtedly are drawn from Biblical or classical sources, but the existence of an independent wild man tradition in Europe seems certain.

Richard Bernheimer, a scholar who studied the European wild man tradition, writes:

"About the wild man's habitat and manner of life medieval authorities are articulate and communicative. It was agreed that he shunned human contact, settling, if possible, in the most remote and inaccessible parts of the forest, and making his bed in crevices, caves, the deep shadow of overhanging branches. In this remote and lonely sylvan home he eked out a living without benefit of metallurgy or even the simplest agricultural lore, reduced to the plain fare of berries and acorns or the raw flesh of animals. At all times he had to be ready to defend his life, for the inner forests teemed with savage beasts real and imaginary, which were wont to attack him. If he was to survive, he had to be the physical equal if not the superior of creatures such as dragons, boars or primeval bulls . . ."

The tradition of the wild man was not spread equally throughout all parts of Europe. It was strongest in mountainous places, parts of Central Europe, and Alpine regions.

Writes Bernheimer: "As described by modern folklorists, the Alpine wild man is a formidable creature. Huge and hairy and mute, and according to some so large that his legs alone have the size of trees. His temper when aroused is terrible and his first impulse that of tearing trespassers to pieces." How like the Abominable Snowman of the Sunday supplements.

Until very recent times it was traditional in some European peasant festivals to have a person dressed in shaggy furs portray the part of the wild man.

The wild man, of course, had to have a mate. But European traditions concerning the wild woman are extremely confused. She is described either as being very beautiful or very ugly—or perhaps both—for she usually possessed the magical ability to change her shape. The wild woman in European tradition is really more of a witch than anything else, and doesn't really fit in with our search for the Abominable Snowman. However, one bit of European wild woman lore does concern us. In her undisguised, ugly form, the wild woman was supposed to have huge sagging breasts which she often slung over her shoulder for convenience. This odd habit comes up in conection with the female Abominable Snowman of the Himalayas.

All these ancient traditions raise a classic chicken-and-egg puzzle about the Abominable Snowman. Are the modern stories merely reflections of the ancient myths, or are the ancient myths themselves reflections of reality? Do the traditions enhance or destroy the credibility of the Abominable Snowman?

Some feel that all the satyrs, fauns, wild men and the rest, represent a mythological embodiment of man's fears and desires concerning life beyond the bounds of civilization. Others think that the stories began as garbled recollections concerning individuals who had gone mad and run away or been driven from the civilized community to live in the woods or mountains. In some parts of Europe a madman was simply called a wild man, and there seemed no distinction between that sort of wild man and any other. In the Bible, King Nebuchadnezzar is supposed to have gone insane and "was driven from men, and did eat grass as oxen, and his body was wet with the dew of heaven, till his hairs were grown like eagles' feathers, and his nails like birds' claws" (Dan. 4:33). Medieval artists depicted Nebuchadnezzar in his mad state as a traditional hair-covered wild man. Even today, many sightings of the Abominable Snowman are often attributed to "some crazed trapper" or "mad Indian."

There is a rare medical condition called hypertrichosis in which a person has long hair all over his body, including his face. In 1556 a hypertrichotic person named Peter Gonzales was born in the Canary Islands. The child was sent as a gift to King Henry II of France, and there he joined the king's collection of dwarfs, giants, and other malformed individuals who have always seemed to amuse kings throughout history.

Since hairiness was believed to be a symptom of wildness, legend has it that the king constructed a cave for his hairy man to live in so that he would not become homesick for the wild life. Gonzales was permitted to marry and several of his children showed the same hairy characteristics. They too became attractions at different European courts. A number of paintings of members of the Gonzales family survive. There is little doubt that with their hairy faces they were striking in appearance, particularly when dressed in formal finery as they were for their portraits.

Hypertrichosis is so rare, occurring about once in every billion persons, that it seems doubtful if it could have had much effect on the origin of the wild man or snowman legends. But the occasional appearance of these hairy individuals throughout history probably helped to keep the legends alive.

There is also the possibility that these hairy wild man legends began, at least in part, as descriptions of genuinely primitive peoples who lived on the outskirts of civilization, and who were gradually pushed back into the most remote and undesirable areas. Such people would always be potentially dangerous, as the American Indians were dangerous to the European settlers. But as these primitive peoples were gradually exterminated, the legends of their ferocity and wildness grew, until they were made to seem half man and half wild beast.

A conservative view is that the stories of the hairy wild man all stem from encounters with known apes or other wild animals. Indeed, there is excellent evidence that no small number of wild man stories are based on just such encounters. In some European traditions the image of the wild man and the image of the bear became interchangeable.

As you might imagine, real monster buffs regard the above explanations as too tame and conventional. They hold that at the very least the wild man-Abominable Snowman is some unknown form of ape. But they are even more strongly attracted to the view that the Abominable Snowman is really some species of "subhuman." Words like "missing link" and "living fossil" are freely tossed about.

The abundance of ancient hairy-wild-man tradition doesn't really resolve the problem either way. For light on the reality of the Abominable Snowman we must turn to modern sources. Let's start where the creature has attained its greatest fame—in the Himalayas.

Monster buffs say that the Himalayas are rich in Abominable Snowman tradition. This claim is hard to support, for much of what has been passed off in the West as genuine Himalayan tradition is frankly suspect.

Let us, for example, look at a story recounted in the early years of this century by Prince Peter of Greece. The prince was doing anthropological research in India and Tibet, and wrote an account of the mysterious Snowman for an Indian newspaper.

Prince Peter told how one of these creatures had been in the habit of invading a village at the mouth of the Jalap Valley in Sikkim and drinking from the water supply. To end the nuisance the villages put out a bowl of strong liquor. The Snowman drank it, fell into a stupor and was captured. Later, however, it revived and escaped. A similar story came from Tibet. There the natives were so upset by the depredations of the Snowmen that after getting them drunk they slaughtered a great number of them. Local authorities had to intervene to stop the massacre of the simple brutes.

Both these stories seem to reflect the old Greek tradition of capturing the wild god Silenus by getting him drunk, a tradition that should have been well known to the Greek prince. Recall how Roger Bacon had reported that this was the method used in Asia for trapping wild men. Again we have the chicken-and-egg puzzle.

A few years ago the Government of Bhutan, a small nation in the Himalayas, issued a series of "Snowman stamps." (Like many small nations Bhutan has almost no postal service, but they still print lots of colorful stamps to sell to foreign collectors.) The stamps are said to show traditional representations of the Abominable Snowman from ancient Bhutanese drawings and paintings. One of the creatures on the stamps is quite obviously an orangutan of the steaming jungles of Java not of the Himalayan snow fields. (It might be well to remember that orangutan is a Malay word that means wild man, for that is how the natives of Java first regarded this large ape.) Another stamp shows what is clearly a mythological demon. It is certainly not any sort of Abominable Snowman, for the creature is depicted as a cyclops with a long tail. Neither the single eye nor the tail has ever figured in Snowman lore.

The point of all this is that no one has really made a serious study of the legends or folklore from the Himalayas concerning the Abominable Snowman. Monster buffs have done just what the Bhutan stamp agency did—lump together traditions concerning many different creatures, real and imaginary, under the popular title of Abominable Snowman lore. We have no right to conclude that belief in the Abominable Snowman or any suchlike creature was widespread in the Himalayas before Snowman hunters from the West began poking about.

Even the words by which the people of the Himalayas are supposed to refer to these manlike creatures are very much in dispute. A thorough philological study of the many names for the Snowman was undertaken by the Indian scholar Sri Swami Pranavananda. He concluded that many of the names which have been attributed to the Abominable Snowman are really references to bears. The word Yeti, most familiar of all the Himalayan words for the Snowman, was meant to describe a thoroughly mythical monster which had nothing whatever to do with the creature for which we are searching.

Naturally enough, monster buffs refused to take this debunking attempt lying down. The writer Ivan Sanderson (who might truly be called the Abominable Snowman's best friend) flayed the Indian philologist, claiming he "created a positive shambles of the Nepalese languages." Sanderson denounced the "specialized methodology" and "crypto-esoteric details" of philological scholarship. He objected particularly to the Indian scholar calling the Nepalese languages Tibetan.

Sanderson then countered with his own expert, Rabbi Yonah N. ibn Aharon, a longtime fighter for exotic causes. Rabbi Aharon flatly contradicted Sanderson by saying, "The proper source for the [Abominable Snowman] words of Nepal is in the Tibetan Lexicon of Jaschke or any of the many excellent Tibetan-Sanskrit dictionaries." Rabbi Aharon compiled a long list of words that run from *Albast,* "One who moves over (lives in) wet places," to *Uli-Bieban,*" Strange or Not-quite-right people who nevertheless walk upright."

Philology is one of the great remaining strongholds of bizarre scholarship. The rules are so loose that one may prove or disprove practically anything. Arguing about names will only lead us deeper into confusion. We must turn to a different sort of evidence—the reports of persons who have claimed to have encountered the mysterious hairy creature of the Himalayas.

There are surprising few recorded encounters between natives of the Himalayan region and the Abominable Snowman. Sanderson lists only nine between 1887 and 1960, and most of these are third- or fourth-hand tales, like the one written up by Prince Peter of Greece of the capture of the Snowman by getting it drunk.

Possibly the best of the native reports comes from the famed sherpa Tensing Norgay, who along with Sir Edmund Hillary first scaled Mt. Everest. Not that Tensing himself had seen the Yeti, but his father had, and Tensing remembered his description of the experience.

The Yeti the elder Tensing encountered was fairly small— only about five feet high—but it had an awful temper. Tensing senior drove the yaks he had been tending into a stone hut to protect them from the enraged Yeti. But the creature began tearing the roof off the hut and throwing stones, like an angry chimpanzee. Finally the elder Tensing built a fire and was able to drive it off.

According to the description, the creature was covered with reddish brown fur, had an apelike face and prominent teeth, and a high conical skull.

The most well-attested native accounts, like those collected by mountaineers H. W. Tilman and Sir John Hunt, speak of a creature five feet or under, and very monkeylike in its activities and appearance. Occasionally, this animal is even reported to drop down and run on all fours when in a hurry.

Sightings by Westerners have been considerably more sensational. The earliest complete report comes from 1920 when it was said that a British explorer, Hugh Knight, encountered a large, blond, bowlegged gorilla carrying a bow and arrow. The report would be a classic but for one small problem: no one has been able to discover who Hugh Knight was or whether he existed at all.

The next sighting is more reliable. It was made in 1925 by N. A. Tombazi, a Greek photographer who was serving as a member of a Royal Geographical Photographic expedition. He was camping at an altitude of some fifteen thousand feet in the mountains of Sikkim, when his porters pointed to something odd moving across the lower slope.

"The intense glare and brightness of the snow prevented me from seeing anything for the first few seconds," Tombazi said. "But I soon spotted the 'object' referred to, about two to three hundred yards away down the valley to the east of our camp. Unquestionably, the figure in outline was exactly like a human being, walking upright and stopping occasionally to uproot or pull at some dwarf rhododendron bushes. It showed up dark against the snow and, as far as I could make out, wore no clothes. Within the next minute or so it had moved into some thick scrub and was lost to view.

"Such a fleeting glimpse, unfortunately, did not allow me to set the telephoto-camera, or even to fix the object carefully with binoculars, but a couple of hours later, during the descent, I purposely made a detour so as to pass the place where the 'man' or 'beast' had been seen. I examined the footprints which were clearly visible on the surface of the snow. They were similar in shape to those of a man, but only six to seven inches long by four inches wide at the broadest part of the foot. The marks of five distinct toes and of the instep were perfectly clear, but the trace of the heel was indistinct, and the little that could be seen of it appeared to narrow down to a point. I counted fifteen such footprints at regular intervals ranging from one-and-a-half to two feet. The prints were undoubtedly of a biped, the order of the spoor having no characteristics whatever of any imaginable quadruped. Dense rhododendron scrub prevented any further investigations as to the direction of the footprints . . . From inquiries I made a few days later . . . I gathered that no man had gone in the direction [of the footprints] since the beginning of the year.

"When I asked the opinion of the Sirdar and the coolies they naturally trotted out fantastic legends of 'Kanchenjunga-demons.' Without in the least believing in these delicious fairy tales myself, notwithstanding the plausible yarns told by the natives, and the references I have come across in many books, I am still at a loss to express any definite opinion. However, I can only reiterate with a sufficient degree of certainty that the silhouette of the mysterious being was unmistakably identical with the outline of a human figure . . ."

Tombazi's account is quoted at length, for although he got only a "fleeting glimpse" of the being, his sighting is probably the best and most responsible on record. In the years that followed, other closer and considerably more colorful encounters with the Yeti were reported. But some of these seem so fantastic, or come from persons whose reliability is so questionable, that they are hard to accept.

Said the British mountaineer Sir John Hunt (the man who planned and led the expedition which sent Hillary and Tensing to the top of Everest): "By far the best evidence of the Yeti which has come to my personal knowledge is that of Professor Tombazi."

Tombazi himself has never forgotten the incident. In 1964 he wrote: "Although nearly forty years have passed, I still carry a vivid impression of the glimpse I caught at the time and I am convinced that the Yeti in the form of a biped and not a quadruped is in existence."

Tombazi's story contains a number of details which are worth remembering. First, Tombazi complained that the press got all the details of his story wrong—a factor which, sadly, we must always keep in mind in an area where "proof" often consists of a stack of newspaper clippings.

Secondly there seemed to be no well-established Yeti or Snowman traditions in the area when Tombazi made his report. He mentions that there were recorded sightings of various kinds, and the "fantastic legends of Kanchenjunga-demons," but this is a far cry from other accounts which indicate that the Yeti is seen so frequently it is almost taken for granted.

Footprints, which constitute some of the most interesting evidence for the Abominable Snowman, are usually thought of as large, even monstrous in size and shape. But those seen by Tombazi were quite small, human in shape, although they were unusually wide.

Then there was the appearance of the creature—it was "exactly like a human being," not at all the lumbering creature so often pictured. Although this "man" or "beast" did not seem to be wearing any clothes, no mention is made of hair either.

What did Tombazi see? Forty years after the sighting he called the thing the Yeti. But immediately after he made his sighting, he had another theory, or at least a guess: "I conjecture then that this 'wild man' may be either a solitary or else a member of an isolated community of pious Buddhist ascetics, who have renounced the world and sought their God in the utter desolation of some high place, as yet undesecrated by the world. However, perhaps, I had better leave these conclusions to ethnological and other experts."

There are Buddhist and Hindu ascetics who seek out the desolation of high places (they can live regularly at altitudes of up to fifteen thousand feet) just as Christian ascetics of the Middle Ages sought out deserts and caves. Such people can endure hardships that would be impossible for the average person. They can and do walk about naked or nearly so in the frigid mountain air. The footprints could have been made by a man wearing clogs or sandals. So Tombazi really could have spotted a wandering ascetic as he had first suspected. The identification is far from certain, but one thing we can be certain about is that Tombazi did not see the huge, hairy monster which is the popular picture of the Abominable Snowman.

Let us go on with the sightings.

In 1944 a South African and two Englishmen sighted a strange creature in the mountains at Liddarwat near Srinagar. "We saw a large animal bounding towards us down the snow-covered ground on the opposite side of the river. Its gait appeared to me to be that of a monkey in a hurry, with all four paws off the ground together . . . It was tawny in colour, with a fringe round its face, was about the size of a man and had a long tail with a tuft on the end, like a lion . . . The Kashmirians said that it was a *bandar* [monkey].

"This strange creature was certainly neither bear nor langur. Can it, wandering alone at these altitudes, have been the Abominable Snowman?"

No, the Kashmirians were probably right. It was a monkey, or rather a langur, for langurs do live at very high altitudes, and fit the description of the large bounding animals almost perfectly, except for the problem of size. The Himalayan langur is rarely more than two and a half feet long, not the sort of animal one would normally describe as large. Still, large is a relative term, and sizes are notoriously hard to judge in the mountains. With this strange and rather ferocious-looking creature bounding around an exaggeration in size is quite understandable. Langur or not, this creature was not the Abominable Snowman, for the Snowman does not have a long tail. A langur does.

A man named Slavomir Rawicz claims that in 1942 he and four companions escaped from a Russian prison camp in Siberia and walked overland to India. Along the way they encountered two Abominable Snowmen. Rawicz's account is very detailed and definite—there is no chance of mistaken identity here—but the story is also quite impossible to confirm in any way.

An even more sensational encounter took place in 1948 when two Norwegian uranium prospectors said they fought a pair of Snowmen. Even the buffs openly label this story as a "suspected fabrication."

In 1956 John Keel, an American writer, claims to have tracked a Snowman for several days, until he finally caught sight of it or something.

In his book *Jadoo* he recorded the sighting this way:

". . . Finally I emerged onto the edge of a sweeping cavity filled with water, where broken trees and decayed bushes poked up like skeletons.

"That was where I saw it!

"Maybe it wasn't a Yeti, I wasn't close enough to be absolutely sure. But something was out there across the lake. Something big, breathtakingly big, and brown and moving swiftly, splashing by a pile of boulders. As I neared them, another brown blur moved out to meet it and together they disappeared beyond the debris of a landfall."

Years later when the author asked Keel about the sighting he was able to add no details, and admitted that the sighting was not really very good.

And that, disappointingly enough, is just about that as far as direct sightings of the Abominable Snowman of the Himalayas are concerned. All the sightings are either of doubtful authenticity, or are explainable as misinterpretations.

Footprints make up more substantial evidence. Far more common than sightings of the actual creature are reports from explorers and mountain climbers of seeing large and vaguely human-shaped footprints in the Himalayan snow fields.

In November 1951, mountaineer Eric Shipton found and photographed a trail of these mysterious footprints on the southwestern slopes of Menlug-tse in the Himalayas. Shipton followed the trail for about a mile until it disappeared on hard ice.

Shipton published several of the photos he had taken. One showed a closeup of the print comparing it to the head of a climber's ice ax. Another showed a print (perhaps the same one) as being about the same size as a climbing boot. A third photograph shows the trail itself. Unfortunately, the photo of the trail is taken from an angle that so distorts the prints that they do not even look like the same footprints that were shown in the closeups. And the Shipton footprints are by far the best available.

As a result of the ambiguous nature of the photographic evidence a controversy over the footprints has simmered for years. They were made by an unknown anthropoid, says one expert. They were made by a bear walking on its hind legs, says another. A third contends that they were made by a line of smaller animals all jumping into the footprints made by the leader of the line. And yet another comments that the footprints were made by a monkey or langur jumping along with all four feet together. (This is just exactly what the creature seen at Liddarwat in 1944 was doing.)

Anyone who has examined animal tracks in the snow, particularly if the tracks are several days old, knows just how deceptive they can be. Prints in the snow can melt and merge in the sunlight and then refreeze at night, so that the next day several small prints have miraculously been turned into a large one of unusual shape.

Melting cannot explain all the unusual prints. Tombazi saw the prints just a few hours after he saw the creature make them. Shipton says that the prints he saw were fresh, and his closeup photo shows the crisp and clear outlines of a freshly made print. But still, melting is undoubtedly a factor in some of the reports of Snowman prints.

Before the okapi, last of the large mammals to be discovered, was ever captured or photographed, scientists were forced to admit its existence when they examined strips of hide from the creature. Do we have any such evidence from the Abominable Snowman?

For a while it seemed as though such evidence did exist in the form of "Yeti scalps." In 1954 a British newspaper, *The Daily Mail,* sponsored an expedition into the Himalayas to find out if the Yeti existed and, if possible, capture and photograph one. No Yeti was seen, but the expedition's work was not limited to tracking down a live specimen. Its members also attempted to investigate the rumors that portions of Yetis, particularly the scalps, were kept as venerated relics in certain Buddhist monasteries.

Expedition members examined three oddly conical "scalps" at three different monasteries. One scalp they immediately declared to be a fake made up from two pieces of hairy skin sewn together. The other two, however, were declared to be genuine. One expedition member had his reservations about the genuineness of the scalps, saying that they could be "made objects." The monks, who reportedly regarded these "scalps" as holy relics, would not allow them to be taken away, although they graciously allowed the scalps to be photographed and even gave the eager explorers a few hairs from the venerated scalps. A few years later an expedition sponsored by Texas oilman Tom Slick was given the same "holy Yeti scalp" treatment.

In 1960 Sir Edmund Hillary, "the Conqueror of Everest," led a huge expedition to the Himalayas. Among the announced purposes of the expedition was to search out information concerning the Yeti. Naturally this sensational goal received a great deal of publicity.

Monster buffs have castigated Sir Edmund's expedition as being too big, too disorganized, too brief, and to prejudiced to find anything of value. But the chief complaint is that not only did the expedition fail to bring back evidence that supported the existence of the Abominable Snowman, it cast strong doubt on some of the evidence that already existed. Hillary was allowed to do more than examine one of the scalps; he was able to bring it back with him, for the examination of Western scientists. It didn't take them long to decide that this "scalp" had been made from the skin of a goatlike animal of the Himalayas, the serow.

Monster buffs responded with an attitude of "we knew it all the time." The scalp, they said, was a "known fake" made in imitation of the real thing. Some even accused Hillary of deliberately chosing a fake scalp in order to debunk the whole Yeti business. His motive was supposed to be pique over not being able to find the Yeti himself.

If the monster buffs knew that this particular scalp was a fake, there is nothing in the literature on the subject prior to 1960 to indicate this. In fact the very scalp that Hillary brought back was cited as a genuine article.

What seems astonishing in retrospect is that anyone could have gotten excited over these "scalps" in the first place. The people of the Himalayas often wear conical caps of felt or fur which look just like the Yeti "scalps." For years pictures of lamas wearing peaked caps and holding peaked "scalps" were published, and no one seemed to notice the resemblance between the two. Some of the "scalps" even had holes in them through which tassels or other decorations must once have been passed.

Monster buffs now assert that many of these caps are imitations of Yeti scalps, and they are often decorated and used for ceremonial purposes. But it is equally reasonable to assume that many of the Yeti stories, which prominently mention the creature's peaked or pointed skull, were inspired by glimpses of men wearing the common headgear of the region. Descriptions and reconstructions of the Yeti often stress that the creature has a ridge of upstanding fur running down the middle of its peaked scalp. Could this in reality be a sewn seam?

One wonders what caused the lamas and others to pass off old fur hats as relics of the Yeti on unsuspecting but enthusiastic visitors. Perhaps it was common politeness. The strangers had, after all, come such a very long way looking for evidence of the Yeti, they could not be allowed to go back disappointed. Perhaps the lamas had some sense of humor. It is pretty funny to think about all those Westerners, awestruck by a fur hat. Or finally, it may simply have begun with a misunderstanding, perhaps this way:

A Western adventurer is visiting a monastery in Nepal. He sees an old and slightly bald peaked fur cap. Knowing that the Yeti is supposed to have a peaked head, he asks excitedly if this could be from the head of a Yeti. The lama, who hasn't the faintest notion of what he is being asked, merely nods agreeably. The adventurer takes this polite nod as confirmation that he is indeed in the presence of a genuine Yeti scalp, and another legend has begun.

What about other concrete evidence? One expedition said it had actually shot a Yeti and taken a photograph of the corpse. The photograph turned out to be of a dead sloth bear. Yeti wrists and hands have been identified as belonging to a variety of known creatures, including man. Other Yeti artifacts are reportedly tucked away in remote monasteries, far from the prying eyes of scientific investigators.

Since the disappointment of the Hillary expedition, interest in the Abominable Snowman of the Himalayas has waned. Attention has shifted to Abominable Snowman-type creatures that have been reported in other parts of the world.

In 1958 the Associated Press reported that a Russian scientist, Dr. A. G. Pronin, had seen the creature in the Pamir Mountains. According to the A.P. report, "Pronin said he twice saw the stooped, hairy creature looking down from an icy peak, but he refused to call it human. It wore no clothes in that harsh climate."

Two Soviet expeditions, one in 1960 and another in 1962, were sent out to find the creature. There was even supposed to be an official "Soviet Study Commission of the Snowman Question."

In 1964 a Russian doctor reported that during World War II he had examined a strange hairy "man" who had been captured as an "enemy agent" in the mountains. Later that same year there were reports out of Russia that strange humanlike skulls had been discovered in Outer Mongolia. One Russian scientist, Professor Boris F. Porschnev, theorized that the Abominable Snowmen were surviving Neanderthal men.

If all these stories are to be believed, then the Russians have built an almost conclusive case for the existence of the Abominable Snowman. But that is the catch: Are they to be believed? As we pointed out in connection with the lake monsters, stories out of the Soviet Union are extraordinarily difficult to confirm. These about the Abominable Snowman remain completely unconfirmed. Until and unless something more solid than a handful of newspaper clips is forthcoming, we are justified in assuming that all these reports are errors, exaggerations, or total fabrications. The same attitude has to be taken toward similar, but even vaguer stories that are said to have originated in China.

For more solid Abominable Snowman evidence we must look much closer to home. This many are reluctant to do. While we might be willing to entertain the idea that a monstrously large and very strange creature can exist in "the mysterious East" or even "behind the Iron Curtain," we find the idea that there might be a similar creature right in our own back yards quite laughable. Yet the monster buffs contend that there are Abominable Snowman-type creatures living in the wilds of Canada and even in California and Wisconsin. Since the Hillary disaster, the buffs have concentrated most of their enthusiasm on New World Abominable Snowmen. In California the creature is called Bigfoot, and in Canada, Sasquatch.

If you have been at all impressed by the Yeti evidence, you have no right to scoff at the Bigfoot or Sasquatch. Evidence for the existence of some sort of hairy manlike creature in California and Canada is as good as it is for the Yeti of the Himalayas. In fact, it is quite a bit better, for we have a brief film of California's Abominable Snowman, or at least a film of something large, strange, and hairy ambling through the California wilderness.

In October 1967 Roger Patterson and Bob Gimlin rode out of the wilderness area northeast of Eureka, California, with the astonishing story that not only had they seen the legendary "Bigfoot" but that they had actually photographed it.

At 3:30 P.M. on October 20, 1967, Patterson and Gimlin spotted: "A sort of man-creature . . . about seven feet tall," walking through the woods about a hundred yards from them. "Gosh darn it . . . And for pity's sakes, she was a female!" Patterson exclaimed. The thing, whatever it was, had "big droopy breasts," and was covered with "short, shiny black hair."

Most monster stories contain a line about how the camera had been left at home, or was out of film or something. But Patterson was well prepared. He was carrying a movie camera loaded with color film, properly set and with the lens cap off, when the creature appeared. Patterson was able to capture a short sequence of it in the distance before it disappeared into the dense woods.

The films are not as clear as one might hope, but they are quite clear enough to rule out any chance of mistaken identity. The thing is not a bear or a cloud of dust or a strangely shaped rock. It is either America's Abominable Snowman, or someone wearing a monkey suit.

The Patterson, Gimlin film made quite a splash. Stills from it were distributed by the wire services and the story was written up in several national magazines, including *Reader's Digest*. But still it had not quite created the sensation Patterson and Gimlin had hoped for. The big money contract from a major magazine fell through. The television and movie promises never materialized. The two were quite frank in expressing their disappointment. One suspects that if the very same photos had been brought back from Nepal, they would have been worth a fortune.

Patterson was no mere idle wanderer who had stumbled across the Bigfoot by accident; he had been looking for it for many years. Patterson, a native of the state of Washington, was apparently unaware of the legends of the Bigfoot which are supposed to abound in the Pacific Northwest. He got his start searching for the creature in December 1959 after reading an article by Ivan Sanderson.

Between 1959 and 1967 Patterson spent a good deal of time searching for the Bigfoot and collecting information about it. He was surprised to find out just how many stories there were which seemed in one way or another to tie in with the concept of an Abominable Snowman in America. The stories not only came from northern California, but from the wilderness areas of Oregon and Washington as well. Some came from quite near his own home of Yakima, Washington.

Patterson wrote: "I have lived in Yakima, Washington, for enty-eight years and had never heard of the hairy apes of t. St. Helens, although it is only seventy miles from home the crow flies."

Near Mt. St. Helens is a place known as "ape canyon." ere, so the story goes, a group of miners was attacked by party of seven-foot apes in 1924. None of the miners was hurt, but they were all badly shaken, and when they returned to town and told their story, a great ape hunt was organized. The searchers found no apes, but reportedly did find some giant manlike footprints, and the badly damaged cabin that had once been inhabited by the miners.

After that sensational beginning, the giant hairy apes were reported in the Mt. St. Helens area more or less regularly. When Jim Carter, an experienced mountaineer and skier, disappeared in ape canyon in May 1950 some related his disappearance to the hairy apes. When searchers went out to look for Carter, they found his trail and were able to determine that he had come down the side of the mountain at breakneck speed, taking chances that no skier of his experience would ever take, "unless something was terribly wrong or he was being pursued," said one of the searchers.

The year 1963 was good for Abominable Snowman sightings in America. According to the *Oregon Journal*, "Three persons driving along a remote mountain road east of the Cascade wilderness area early Sunday say they saw a ten-foot, white, hairy figure moving rapidly along the roadside. It was caught in the headlights as their car passed, but they were too frightened to turn around to investigate . . . Another Portland woman and her husband fishing on the Lewis River south of Mt. St. Helens saw a huge beige figure, 'bigger than any human,' along the bank of the river. As they watched, it moved into a thicket with a lumbering gait."

Aside from the sightings, many tracks were found, photographed, and preserved in plaster casts. The tracks were distinctly human in shape, as contrasted with the rather ape-like appearance of many of the Yeti footprints photographed in the Himalayas. The footprints of the Bigfoot, appropriately enough, were huge, ranging anywhere from seventeen to twenty-two inches in length.

It was finding footprints, rather than encounters with the creature itself, that really rekindled interest in the Bigfoot in California. In October 1958, members of a road crew working in a mountainous wilderness area of Humboldt County in northern California reported seeing strange large tracks around their camp. One of the men, a tractor driver named Jerry Crew, made plaster casts of a pair of the prints and showed them to Andrew Genzoli, editor of the *Humboldt Times* in Eureka, California. Editor Genzoli was impressed and ran a major front-page story on Crew's discovery. Then the balloon went up. Not only was the story picked up by the national wire services and a number of national magazines, it also stimulated a flow of accounts from others who claimed to have seen monstrous footprints, or the Bigfoot itself.

Interest in the Bigfoot continues to this day. A small but dedicated group of buffs exchange information through the "Bigfoot Bulletin," a mimeographed sheet that collects news of sightings and other "Bigfoot events" from all parts of the nation and the world. In addition, the Humboldt State College Library at Arcata, California, in the heart of California's "Bigfoot country," collects material about the creature, and presented a special "Bigfoot Display" in 1969. There is a

Bigfoot Drive-in in Oakhurst, California, and a Bigfoot statue at Willow Creek, California.

Individual hunters and adventurers and even a couple of full-scale expeditions (including one sponsored by Texas oilman Tom Slick, who backed a Himalayan Yeti expedition) have set out to capture the Bigfoot. There were a few sightings, many footprints, odd noises, and many tales of eerie feelings of "being watched," but no Bigfoot, dead or alive, was brought out of the wilderness, and until the Patterson film of 1967 there were no pictures, either. (A set of fuzzy photos of dubious authenticity and mysterious origin were printed in a San Francisco paper in 1965, but they were not taken too seriously.) The well-equipped expeditions were no more successful than was Lee Trippett, an electronics engineer from Eugene, Oregon, who set out to capture the creature by influencing its subconscious through extrasensory perception.

It is difficult to determine whether there is a genuine tradition of apelike wild men living in the mountains of the Pacific Northwest. Monster buffs say that such creatures were well known to the Indians under a variety of different names, depending on which tribe was describing the creature. The most commonly used name seemed to be *Oh-Mah*. But the stories of the *Oh-Mah* are quite vague, and for the most part quite recent. *Oh-Mah* may simply mean demon or evil spirit of the wilderness. Enthusiasts looking for a respectable ancestry for the Bigfoot have adopted this convenient label.

The oldest known published account of a Bigfoot-type of creature in the United States is contained in a pamphlet about Siskiyou County, California, dated January 2, 1886:

"I do not remember to have seen any reference to the 'Wild Man' which haunts this part of the country, so I shall allude to him briefly. Not a great while since, Mr. Jack Dover, one of our most trustworthy citizens, while hunting saw an object

standing one hundred and fifty yards from him picking berries or tender shoots from the bushes. The thing was of a
gigantic size—about seven feet high—with a bull dog head,
short ears and long hair; it was also furnished with a beard,
and was free from hair on such parts of its body as is common among men. Its voice was shrill, or soprano, and very
human, like that of a woman in great fear. Mr. Dover could
not see its footprints as it walked on hard soil. He aimed his
gun at the animal or whatever it is, several times, but because
it was so human would not shoot . . . A number of people
have seen it and all agree in their descriptions, except some
make it taller than others . . ."

The buffs list this intriguing item about a giant wild man
with evidence for the Bigfoot, but it may not properly belong there. The creature is described as long-haired and
bearded, but the body was hairless. The most outstanding
characteristic of the Bigfoot and all other Abominable Snowman-type creatures is their hairy body.

The oldest known published record of an Abominable
Snowman-type creature in the Western Hemisphere comes
from Canada. It is not only the oldest record, but one of the
most significant, for it concerns the capture of one of the
creatures alive.

The story appeared in the Victoria, B.C., newspaper, *The
Daily British Colonist*, and monster buffs can almost quote it
from memory:

"YALE, B.C., July 3, 1884. In the immediate vicinity of
No. 4 tunnel, situated some 20 miles above this village, are
bluffs of rock which have hitherto been insurmountable, but
on Monday morning last were successfully scaled by Mr.
Onderdonk's employees on the regular train from Lytton.
Assisted by Mr. Costeron, the British Columbia Express
Company's messenger, a number of gentlemen from Lytton
and points east of that place, after considerable trouble and

perilous climbing captured a creature who may truly be called half man and half beast. 'Jacko' as the creature has been called by its capturers, is something of the gorilla type standing about 4 feet 7 inches in height and weighing 127 pounds. He has long, black, strong hair and resembles a human being with one exception, his entire body, excepting his hands (or paws) and feet are covered with glossy hair about one inch long. His forearm is much longer than a man's forearm and he possesses extraordinary strength, as he will take hold of a stick and break it by wrenching or twisting it, which no man living could break in the same way. Since his capture he is very reticent, only occasionally uttering a noise which is half bark and half growl. He is, however, becoming daily more attached to his keeper, Mr. George Telbury, of this place, who proposes shortly starting for London, England, to exhibit him. His favorite food so far is berries and he drinks fresh milk with evident relish . . ."

The story goes on to describe how Jacko was first sighted and then captured after "five minutes of perilous climbing."

This intriguing story is the beginning, but unfortunately also the end of Jacko as far as the public records are concerned. Did Mr. Telbury take Jacko to London? Did the creature die before leaving the country? What happened to the remains? Monster buffs have searched newspaper files in British Columbia but have been able to come up with no answers to these questions. However, in 1945 a reporter interviewed a man in Lytton, B.C., who said he remembered seeing Jacko when he was young.

For all its isolated and enigmatic quality the story of the capture of Jacko has a plausible ring to it. Assuming it is not a complete hoax, what might Jacko have been? To the buffs he could be nothing other than an Abominable Snowman—a young one, of course, which accounts for his relatively small size.

But from the very start a more probable explanation was advanced. Jacko was an ape. The headline on the original newspaper story calls Jacko "A British Columbia Gorilla." But the description makes it far more likely that he was a chimpanzee. Now, how on earth did a chimpanzee (or any other ape for that matter) get to British Columbia? The stock answer is that it escaped from a traveling carnival. The "wild animal escaped from a traveling carnival explanation" has become such a hoary cliché that it is hard to repeat with a straight face. Mere mention of it will start monster buffs hooting in derision. Still, it could have happened.

But it is really not necessary to ring in a traveling carnival. Jacko might have been someone's pet; perhaps he belonged to a sailor who picked him up in Africa. Yale, where Jacko was captured, is on the Frazer River. The river flows into the channel between Vancouver Island and the mainland of British Columbia. This channel area contains some of the best port facilities in Canada. Chimps make winning and affectionate pets when young, but as they grow older they become unpredictable and even dangerous. Jacko's measurements are those of a large adult male chimpanzee. Jacko might have broken away from his master, or even been deliberately liberated by someone who suddenly found that his exotic pet was just too much to handle. A chimpanzee would be able to survive in British Columbia during the summer, at least for a short time. Jacko was captured in July. The creature's attachment to its new keeper, which is stressed in the newspaper account, indicates that Jacko was not entirely wild and unused to human company.

The men who captured Jacko seemed unaware of any tradition of wild men in Canada. But according to monster buffs the tradition of the hairy wild giant is strong among the Canadian Indians. They call him the Sasquatch, and this name is now generally applied to all Abominable Snowman-type creatures reported north of the Canadian border.

As usual, the name presents problems. It first appeared in print in the 1920s and 1930s in the stories of a British Columbia writer, J. W. Burns. Burns had been a teacher at an Indian reservation, but it is not clear how much of the information in his Sasquatch stories came from Indian legends and how much from his own imagination. Besides, Burns's Sasquatch was really a giant Indian who lived in the wilderness, not some sort of huge subhuman. This Sasquatch was called hairy because he had long hair on his head, not because he was covered with hair.

Burns's character was quite popular. There was a Sasquatch Inn near the town of Harrison, B.C., and the town had even held a local celebration called "Sasquatch Days." The celebration was to be revived as part of British Columbia's centennial. As a publicity stunt a great Sasquatch hunt was planned. This captured the public's imagination and resulted in exactly what the originators had hoped for, a great deal of publicity. The projected hunt never took place; in fact, it had never been meant seriously. But one unlooked-for result of all the publicity was that people began to take the idea of the Sasquatch very seriously indeed.

One spectacular or well-publicized monster report usually stimulates a flood of new sightings or unlocks recollections of old ones. In the story of the Sasquatch the key report was that of William Roe. It was made public by John Green, publisher of the *Agassiz-Harrison Advance*, a small newspaper in British Columbia's "Sasquatch country," and one of the backers of the Sasquatch celebration. According to Roe's sworn statement, he encountered a strange creature in October 1955 "near a little place called Tete Jaune Cache, British Columbia, about 80 miles west of Jasper, Alberta."

Of the encounter Roe said, ". . . My first impression was of a huge man about six feet tall, almost three feet wide, and probably weighing somewhere near 300 pounds. It was covered from head to foot with dark brown, silver-tipped hair . . . the hair that covered it, leaving bare only the parts of its face around the mouth, nose and ears, made it resemble an animal as much as a human. None of this hair, even on the back of its head, was longer than an inch."

Roe considered shooting "the thing," but decided it was just too human, and he would never forgive himself. And so William Roe's Sasquatch lumbered back into the obscurity from whence it had come.

When Green published Roe's account it was met with the expected incredulity. But it was also followed by a trickle of reports from people who had experiences which in one way or another seemed to confirm Roe's encounter. Green's office became sort of a clearinghouse for such reports, and in a few years he had collected enough of them to be able to publish a book on the subject.

Hands down, the most sensational report he received, and probably the most sensational firsthand account in the whole history of Abominable Snowman lore, came from Albert Ostman, a retired logger and construction worker. Ostman said that back in 1924 he had not only seen a Sasquatch, but he had actually been kidnapped by the creature and lived for several days with a Sasquatch family in the wilds of British Columbia before making his escape back to civilization.

The Sasquatches, as Ostman tells the story, were more human than animal, but lived on an extremely primitive level. They did not know the use of fire, had no tools, and lived by gathering plants. But they did possess a sort of rudimentary language.

Monster buffs hardly know what to make of this story. In the years that followed its publication some of them have made pilgrimages to see Ostman. Many have come away convinced of the literal truth of the old man's tale, others have reservations. Those outside of the circle of monster enthusiasts usually reject such a story out of hand. Yet, if it had come from Nepal, and the teller had been a sherpa or a lama rather than a retired construction worker, it might well have become a classic.

If half-century-old kidnappings seem a bit too much, perhaps you would be more interested in the experience of John Bringsli of Nelson, B.C. In October 1960 Bringsli was out picking huckleberries when he spotted, ". . . this great beast. It was standing about fifty feet away on a slight rise in ground, staring at me . . . It was seven to nine feet tall, with long legs and short, powerful arms and with hair covering its body . . . It had very wide shoulders and a flat face with ears flat against the side of its head. It looked more like a big, hairy ape."

Bringsli and the beast stared at one another for about two minutes. Then Bringsli took off back to his car, and drove away as fast as the 1931 coupé could carry him. When he returned later, accompanied by gun-toting friends, the thing was gone. The only evidence around was one strange footprint.

Legends and stories of a similar nature can be found in South America, Africa, and of course from many parts of Asia. But those places are a long way from here. British Columbia is still pretty wild and northern California—well, you know *anything* can happen in California. But the hairy monster has popped up in more prosaic places. Newspaper accounts of encounters with strange hairy creatures have been gathered from Tennessee, Alabama, and even Indiana.

Recently Wisconsin had its own Abominable Snowman flap. A group of hunters reported a hairy manlike creature in a place called Deltox Marsh. Ivan Sanderson and Bernard Heuvelmans examined a set of tracks that the creature supposedly had made, but they were disappointed. The tracks looked "suspiciously man made."

"But," says Sanderson, "perhaps we went to look at these tracks in too skeptical a mood and our appraisal may have been prejudiced."

In judging evidence for and against the Abominable Snowman a good deal depends on your mood. For a moment, let us approach the evidence in the best and most enthusiastic of moods. Let us consider that this hairy manlike thing really exists. What is it?

The Abominable Snowman almost certainly has to be a primate—a member of the order to which man and apes belong. One noted zoologist openly speculated that the Yeti of the Himalayas might be some sort of unknown giant ape. For this public speculation he was chided by his cautious colleagues. But monster buffs are not too happy with the theory either. Although the discovery of an unknown giant ape would be a sensation, it is far too tame for the buffs. If the Abominable Snowman is anything it has to be some sort of subhuman—a "missing link" between man and ape.

A whole range of subhumans, from dwarfs to giants, has been postulated to explain the variations in sightings. But the majority of interest has, naturally enough, centered on the hairy giants. A problem is that for most of their evolutionary history primates have been small. Man is an unusually large primate, and the gorilla which can weigh over five hundred pounds is the veritable giant of the order. But there are a few bits of bones and teeth that indicate that there once may have been primates of truly gigantic stature.

In the 1930s Ralph von Koenigswald, a Dutch geologist and paleontologist, was browsing through the cabinets of "dragon teeth" in a Chinese drugstore in Hong Kong, when he came upon a very unusual tooth. As we have already noted, these "dragon teeth" were usually the fossil teeth of extinct animals, so Chinese drugstores were of great interest to paleontologists. The particular tooth that von Koenigswald had found was in poor shape, and the roots were missing, but still he was able to identify it as a tooth from a primate. It was far and away the largest primate tooth that anyone had ever seen. Over the next few years von Koenigswald collected two other teeth from the creature. He named it *Gigantopithecus* or "giant ape."

Von Koenigswald showed his collection to another paleontologist, the brilliant and often controversial Franz Weidenreich. Weidenriech decided that the teeth were not those of a giant ape, but of a giant man, "and should therefore have been named *Gigantanthropus* (giant man) and not *Gigantopithecus* (giant ape)."

Weidenreich thought the teeth could be related to a puzzling fragment of jawbone von Koenigswald had found in Java. The jawbone also seemed to indicate that the owner had been a human of gigantic stature. Von Koenigswald had given the Java giant the name *Meganthropus*. The teeth of the Chinese giant were one third larger than those of the Java giant.

Weidenreich came to a sensational conclusion. "I believe that all these [giant] forms have to be ranged back in the human line and that the human line leads to giants, the farther back it is traced . . . In other words the giants may be directly ancestral to man."

This theory was of great interest to monster buffs, and for a while they were ready to claim that the Yeti and the Chinese Giant were one and the same. But then Chinese paleontologists spoiled the fun by discovering three complete jawbones of *Gigantopithecus*. From examination of these more complete remains the scientists decided that the creature definitely was an ape, and probably no more manlike than the chimpanzee. Worse yet, the size of the teeth was misleading. *Gigantopithecus,* they said, was really no larger than a large gorilla. It was a big ape, but no nine-foot giant. Some monster buffs denounce the Chinese scientists as a group of fools and incompetents. They say the creature is human, a giant, and the Abominable Snowman, no matter what the Chinese may say.

But ape or man, the *Gigantopithecus* finds do apparently place a very large two-legged and presumably hairy creature in Asia, at least roughly in the same area in which the most famous Abominable Snowman sightings have taken place. If *Gigantopithecus* or something like it survived until the present day it could quite easily account for all the stories of the Abominable Snowman.

Evidence for the survival of some sort of large apes in China is tantalizing. As far as we know *Gigantopithecus* became extinct at least seven hundred thousand years ago. But around 400 B.C. the philosopher Hsun-Tzu recorded that an ape about the size of a man and covered with hair lived in the Yellow River Valley. What is more, he noted that this ape stood erect. Somewhere around the time of the birth of Christ there is a record of apes in northern Sinkiang province near Tibet. This is not only very close to classic Yeti territory, it is also near the place where the giant panda was able to hide from science until the twentieth century. So large and striking-looking animals are hard to find there. A Tibetan book, published in Peking, contains a picture of what looks like an upright ape. (This picture wound up on one of the Bhutanese Snowman stamps.) The caption reads: "The wild man lives in the mountains, his habitat is close to that of the bear, his body resembles that of a man, and he has enormous strength. His meat may be eaten to treat mental diseases and his gall cures jaundice." This last bit of advice is not very helpful. The odd medical theories of the day should not prejudice us, for in other ways this book's treatment of this "wild man" is quite realistic and matter-of-fact.

Human evolution has not been a simple straight-line process. Although all the human beings living today are members of a single species (*Homo sapiens*), during other periods of human development there were several different species of human or near-human types living in the same place at the same time. In China, for example, during the middle of the Pleistocene period, there lived the famous beetling-browed Peking man. But Chinese scientists have now discovered that there was another even more primitive type alive at the same time. This new find is classified as *Homo erectus lantiensis*, "Lan-t'ien Man." In recent years Africa too has yielded the fossils of a bewildering array of men and near-men who seem to have lived as neighbors for thousands of years.

In Europe the celebrated Neanderthal man was a contemporary of "modern" man. At one time it was believed that Neanderthal man was some sort of apish evolutionary dead end that had lived only in Europe during the Ice Age. We now know that Neanderthal or Neanderthal types were widespread. Moreover, they were closely related to modern man; most authorities classify Neanderthal man as a subspecies of modern man.

At the end of the Ice Age, Neanderthal man, who seems to have been flourishing, died out. Why? The usual argument is that he was somehow "unfit" for survival, but it does not fit the known facts, for Neanderthal man seemed extraordinarily well fitted for survival. True, he had heavy brow ridges and big teeth, but survival is not based on beauty. Neanderthal man had a large brain, larger even than ours; his tools and weapons were equal to or better than those of early "modern" man. Besides, Neanderthal man had already survived the rigors of several glacial advances and retreats. Why would this hardy fellow suddenly become "unfit"?

Another theory holds that our ancestors evolved somewhere in the Middle East and then migrated to Europe and other areas occupied by the Neanderthals. As we are painfully aware, we are an aggressive species. Our ancestors, the theory runs, were no less so—they exterminated the peaceful Neanderthals and all other near-human types.

Is it possible that this ancient war between two closely related types of human beings is reflected in a symbolic way in the Biblical struggle between the twins Esau and Jacob? Some monster buffs think so. And they carry further the theory of warfare between types of men. The victory of *Homo sapiens*—our ancestors—was not complete. The surviving Neanderthals fled from their conquerors and took refuge in high and inaccessible places. Here they managed to maintain a precarious survival by staying out of the way of our bloodthirsty ancestors. Ultimately, the theory runs, the origins of the refugees was forgotten by the outside world. The surviving Neanderthals succeeded so well in hiding themselves that their very existence was in doubt. They became incorporated in the wild man legends and ultimately into the modern legends of the Abominable Snowman.

According to some reports the Russians definitely think that the Yeti is some sort of prehistoric man. A 1964 report quotes a Professor Porschnev as saying that two hominoid skulls were found in Mongolia: "The skulls were found exactly where scores of people, from shepherds and milkmaids, to local authorities, have reported seeing these terrifying and remarkable bipeds." A Mongolian scientist B. Rinchen went even further reporting that these people called the *almas* had been squeezed into about a 385-square-mile area. As usual, there has been nothing to back up these reports.

There are drawbacks to the attractive theory that Abominable Snowman—wild man legends originated with a primitive people (aside from the obvious drawback that there is not a scrap of material evidence to indicate that the theory is true). In the first place, the near-human types were not giants. Neanderthal man was bulky, but not as tall as modern man. *Meganthropus* of Java and some of the near-men that lived in Africa were quite large, but there is no evidence that there has ever been an ape or man nine or twelve feet tall. In fact, there are a number of sound anatomical arguments which say that a two-legged creature of that size would be unable to walk upright. The bipedal gait is a strain even for the human being. The evidence for this is the amount of back trouble we suffer from.

Identifying the Abominable Snowman as a primate is particularly difficult in the Western Hemisphere. We have some of the best Snowman stories but no fossil evidence that any creature remotely resembling the Abominable Snowman has ever existed in this part of the world. There are no fossil men, apes, or man-apes. Indeed, the only large primate we know of that has ever existed in the Western Hemisphere is *Homo sapiens*, a fairly recent immigrant. (The monkeys of South America are primates, but they are generally small, and not on the branch of primate evolution that led to the great apes and man.)

The absence of fossil evidence can be reasoned away by assuming that both man and Abominable Snowman migrated from Asia across the Bering Strait land bridge at about the same time. Perhaps man even chased the more peaceful hairy giant across the land bridge.

North America would have been a pretty good place for Abominable Snowmen. Until modern times the continent has had a thin *Homo sapiens* population. After the end of the Ice Age there were few large predators on the continent to kill off this shy giant. The Abominable Snowman should have prospered. Why then did he not leave behind a single bone or tooth by which he could be identified?

He may have, say the monster buffs. There are rumors of giant jawbones, human in appearance, that are stored unidentified in the basements of small museums. Another jawbone was reportedly kept by a trapper and his wife for twenty years until it was finally destroyed in a fire which burned down their home. In the end, however, the bones of the Sasquatch or Bigfoot have proved just as elusive as the bones of the Yeti of the Himalayas.

But who needs bones or scalps when you can get the whole Abominable Snowman or missing link or what have you frozen in a block of ice? In May 1969 Sanderson and Heuvelmans said they had examined a strange hairy "man-thing" that was being displayed at a sideshow somewhere "west of the Mississippi." Whatever it is was frozen inside a big block of ice, so photographs show it only in hazy outline. But artists' renderings from these foggy pictures make the thing look like the original wolf-man himself.

The thing was brought to the United States from somewhere in the Orient under mysterious circumstances. Despite the fact that it is supposed to have been on public display "Bozo's" (for that is what Sanderson has nicknamed it) present whereabouts are equally mysterious. The author's request to examine it were politely turned aside.

When the Smithsonian Institution asked to X-ray the block of ice the carnival manager would not let them. He announced that the mysterious owner of the monster had withdrawn it from exhibition and that it would never again be shown to the public. To fill the gap the carnival had prepared a model of the original which would henceforth be on display. Sanderson contends that the model looks different than the thing he and Heuvelmans originally examined.

Fake monsters are, of course, nothing new. Around the

turn of the century the Cardiff Giant, a stone fake "discovered" in New York State, had quite a run. As we have seen, Jenny Hanivers and "Baby Dragons" have all been fashioned to capture the credulous. By sticking a monster inside a block of ice, thus well away from close examination, a hoaxer would have made things quite easy on himself. Unless Bozo is delivered up to some reliable scientific institution, we will simply have to regard him as a latter-day Cardiff Giant.

The interesting thing about a story like this is that it will never die. Thirty years from now monster buffs will be repeating how the frozen body of an Abominable Snowman was shipped to America where it was examined by two noted scientists who declared it to be the genuine article.

Now that we have speculated about what the Abominable Snowman might be if he does exist, we might spend a moment thinking about what he might be if he does not exist. The statement is not meant as a paradox, for if there is no real hairy giant off in the wilds, we have an enormous number of stories and legends to account for, from hairy Enkidu of the ancient Gilgamesh Epic to the current Bigfoot and Sasquatch sightings.

In this study of wild man mythology of the Middle Ages Richard Bernheimer notes:

"It appears that the notion of the wild man must respond and be due to a persistent psychological urge. We may define this urge as the need to give external expression and symbolically valid form to the impulses of reckless physical self-assertion which are hidden in all of us, but are normally kept under control. These impulses, which are strongest and most aggressive in the very young, are restricted slowly, as the child learns to come to terms with a civilized environment which will not tolerate senseless noise, wanton destruction, and uncalled for interference with its activities. But the repressed desire for such unhampered self-assertion persists and may finally be projected outward as the image of a man who is free as the beasts, able and ready to try his strength without regard for the consequences to others, and therefore able to call up forces which his civilized brother has repressed in his effort at self-control. In contrast to civilized man, the wild man is a child of nature, upon whose hidden resources he can depend, since he has not removed himself from its guidance and tutelage."

The wild man, Abominable Snowman, Yeti, Sasquatch, Bigfoot, or what have you is a profoundly anti-establishment figure today. His very existence is an affront to science, indeed to civilization itself. To everyone who resents the rigid rules of science and civilization (and in some ways, who doesn't?) the hairy monster has enormous appeal. He is also a shining goal for the frustrated adventurer. One time a man could prove his masculinity by big game hunting. But there is precious little big game left, and more and more people regard big game hunting as a barbarous anachronism. But to shoot or capture the Abominable Snowman, and to do it in the name of science—now there would be a feat.

These psychological reasons, rather than any weight of evidence, are, I believe, the reasons for the Abominable Snowman's eternal popularity.

Monsters from the Past

The extinction of the species is much talked about today. But historically extinction is a new idea and one that man has found difficult to accept. Thomas Jefferson, who was a natural scientist of no small accomplishment, and a very advanced thinker for his time, wrote, "Such is the economy of nature, that no instance can be produced of her having permitted any one race of her animals to become extinct; of her having formed any link in her great work so weak as to be broken."

Jefferson collected the fossil bones of huge animals that had once roamed the area near his home in Virginia. Clearly they no longer lived in Virginia, but he assumed that these giants did live somewhere in the world, probably in the unexplored regions of the American West.

The West was explored but the elephants and other giants whose bones Jefferson had collected were not found living there. Today many persist in the belief that some creatures of

171

monstrous size and appearance which are generally thought to be extinct do survive somewhere. The focus of attention has shifted from the now thoroughly explored American West to the jungles of Central Africa, remote islands in the Pacific, and the dark and forbidding taiga forests of Siberia.

In any discussion of the possibility of monstrous survivors one will sooner or later—usually sooner—be confronted with the case of *Latimeria chalumnae*, the coelacanth. *Latimeria* is a big, ugly, heavily scaled, bulgy-eyed fish with fins that look strikingly like rudimentary legs. Indeed, *Latimeria* is a member of that group of fishes which first crawled out of the sea onto the land. But it is not *Latimeria's* unique evolutionary position that makes it important to this discussion. Its signficance is that *Latimeria* is generally conceded to be the most famous of the "living fossils."

The term "living fossil" has been used by popular-science writers for years, yet it inevitably causes a certain amount of unnecessary confusion. To the man in the street "living fossil" too often conjures up supernatural associations. It does, after all, sound like "living dead," a popular term for zombies, ghosts, vampires, and the like.

Living fossils are a good deal more prosaic. Any animal or plant that has existed without much evolutionary change for a very long time might properly be considered a living fossil. The horseshoe crab first appeared in Triassic times, two hundred million years ago. It is obviously an evolutionary success, for it has not only existed but also flourished almost unchanged from that day to this. It is a proper living fossil.

But used that way, the term is a little too broad to be of much use to us. Bernard Heuvelmans has usefully narrowed the term further. "It is generally agreed to limit 'living fossils' to very small groups of survivors which have perpetuated themselves throughout the ages while larger groups have been undergoing vast changes and still giving birth to new types."

A good example of this sort of living fossil is the tuatara, a rare and largish lizard that lives only in New Zealand. The tuatara is the sole survivor of the order Rhynchocephalia, which evolved before the great dinosaurs appeared.

But because of the dramatic and well-known details of its discovery *Latimeria* has become the most celebrated and most commonly cited of the living fossils. The case of *Latimeria* has become Exhibt A in all arguments supporting the possibility of the survival of monsters from the past.

On December 22, 1938, a fishing boat netted an unusually lively and unusually unattractive fish about eighteen miles off the southern coast of Africa. None of the fishermen had ever seen anything like it before. The fish was five feet long, covered with large, steel-blue scales, and possessed prominent deep-blue eyes. It remained alive out of the water for almost three hours, snapping viciously at anyone who approached it.

The captain of the fishing boat knew that he had a rare prize but by the time he was able to get the strange fish to the local museum, it was quite dead. By the time any experts got around to looking at it there was nothing left to look at but skin. The rest of the fish had become so putrid that it had to be discarded. But from the skin and from sketches made of the complete specimen the fish was identified as a coelacanth, a member of a once numerous group, which, from all fossil evidence available, had been extinct for at least seventy million years.

A substantial reward was offered for another coelacanth specimen, but no one claimed that reward for fourteen years. However, in recent years specimens of *Latimeria* have turned up more regularly, and the living fossil has even been photographed swimming underwater. *Latimeria* has turned out to be not nearly as rare as first believed. It had been seen by fishermen many times, but none of them thought there was anything unusual about it. Living fossil or not, to the fishermen it was just another big ugly fish.

The significance of *Latimeria* is not that it survived, but that this large and unusual-looking fish existed for so long in waters that were fished fairly regularly, without ever having come to the attention of scientists. If it can happen to *Latimeria*, say the monster buffs, why couldn't it happen to other animals as well?

First and foremost among the candidates for survival are those greatest monsters of earth's past, the dinosaurs. Dinosaurs that have lived on in the depths of the jungle or on some remote Pacific Island are stock characters in certain types of science fiction horror films. Usually the "dinosaurs" in these films are ordinary little lizards, perhaps with a horn or two pasted on to make them look more exotic, and then blown up by trick photography.

But let's not be put off by this sort of publicity. We should try to consider the possibility of dinosaurian survival with an open mind. To do this we must begin at the beginning. What is a dinosaur? Despite its Hollywood image and despite the fact that the word dinosaur itself means "terrible lizard," dinosaurs are not just big lizards. They are not lizards at all. Dinosaur is a general term that refers to a large and extremely diverse group of terrestrial reptiles. Dinosaurs ranged from smallish birdlike creatures to the largest land animals that have ever existed.

As far as science is concerned, all the many, many species of dinosaurs died out by the end of the Mesozoic era, some seventy million years ago. When we wish to refer to something clumsy, outsized, ineffective, and obviously headed straight for oblivion we call it a dinosaur, as though the dinosaur were some sort of horrible example of evolutionary failure. Nothing could be further from the truth. Dinosaurs

were the dominant life forms on land for nearly one hun[
million years. Balance that record against the fact that [
in one form or another has been around for a mere million
million and a half years, and we are already worrying, with
some justification, about our own possible extinction. We
must conclude that in no sense were the dinosaurs evolutionary failures.

The first mammals and the first dinosaurs evolved at about
the same time. But while the dinosaurs grew and flourished,
the mammals remained tiny, and insignificant, probably because they could not compete successfully with the superbly
adapted giant reptiles.

But then, after an almost inconceivably long reign as kings
of the earth, all the dinosaurs died out, quite suddenly it
seems. Dinosaur fossils are common in rocks from the Cretaceous period, but they are entirely absent from the rocks of
the Paleocene, the very next geological epoch.

Geological periods are measured in blocks of millions or
tens of millions of years, and so the suddenness of the disappearance of the dinosaurs may be more apparent than real.
They may have gone into a decline and become extinct over
a period of ten or fifteen million years. Indeed many types of
dinosaurs had become extinct and were replaced by other
kinds of dinosaurs during the Mesozoic era, the time of dinosaurian dominance.

So we do not know for certain if the final decline and death
of the dinosaurs came slowly or not. The geological record
makes it look freakishly abrupt. Dr. Edwin H. Colbert of
the American Museum of Natural History, and one of the
world's leading experts on diniosaurs says: "The problem of
extinction is one to which we return, time and again, even
though very little is known about it. The most hardheaded
blasé geologist is more often than not apt to get excited when

he becomes involved in a discussion of the extinction of the dinosaurs."

Over the years everyone from respected scientists to raving crackpots have offered theories to explain the death of the dinosaurs. No single theory seems really satisfactory and none has won general acceptance.

Great catastrophes, like the Biblical flood, which were once used to explain all extinctions, no longer find much favor among scientists. "Catastrophes," grumbles Colbert, "are the mainstays of people who have very little knowledge of the natural world; for them the invocation of catastrophes is an easy way to explain great events."

Besides, if the extinction of the dinosaurs was caused by a catastrophe it was a very particular sort of catastrophe. The dinosaurs died, so did the pterosaurs and other flying reptiles and the marine reptiles such as the ichthyosaurs, mosasaurs, and plesiosaurs. But many other reptiles were untouched by whatever it was that happened. Turtles, for example, lived side by side with the dinosaurs. They plodded their way right through the Mesozoic, unscathed and unchanged until the present day. So did the crocodiles and many varieties of lizards. (Snakes represent a relatively recent, and highly successful addition to the reptile clan.)

In the last few years some astronomers have advanced a new view concerning the extinction of the dinosaurs. The theory might be called cosmic catastrophism. These astronomers propose that something—perhaps the explosion of a nearby supernova, perhaps the weakening of the earth's protective magnetic shield—resulted in a greatly increased bombardment of radiation from space. This radiation affected the dinosaurs' reproductive cells and caused sterility which quickly and completely spelled the doom of the great reptiles.

The theory is attractive, probably because it sounds new,

and in this era of great progress in astronomy it is fashionable. The astronomers have calculated the probability of supernovas, and speculated at great length on the possible causes and effects of a weakening of the magnetic shield. But in the end both of these ideas are unsatisfactory in the same way that earlier catastrophic theories were unsatisfactory, they fail to explain the highly selective nature of the extinction. One can understand how the exposed dinosaurs succumbed, while the tiny mammals, who presumably lived in holes in the ground were protected from the most damaging effects of the radiation storm. But the theory does not explain why the giant marine reptiles died, and the turtles and crocodiles survived.

Equally unsatisfactory is the most popular theory—that some sort of world-wide climatic change brought about the doom of the dinosaurs and other great reptiles. We do know that during the long reign of the dinosaurs, the earth's surface features, climate and vegetation, did change very dramatically. But the dinosaurs proved quite adaptable and easily survived these changes. Even assuming some sort of major but unknown change of climate at the end of the Mesozoic era we still face the problem of why every single dinosaur died out. Major climate changes could undoubtedly have a catastrophic effect on some of the dinosaurs, particularly the largest of them. These giants would have been particularly vulnerable to changes in moisture and vegetation. But not all dinosaurs were giants. Surely some of the smaller ones should have been able to survive as well as the crocodiles and the turtles.

But they didn't. Says Dr. Colbert: "Not one of them survived into a later geological age, as is amply proved by the fact that during almost a century and a half of paleontological exploration, the wide world over, no trace of a dinosaur bone or tooth has ever been found in any post-Cretaceous rocks, not even the earliest of them. The proof of the geologic record on this score is irrefutable."

"Irrefutable?" Well, perhaps, but many have spent a good deal of time and effort trying to refute it.

During the nineteenth century, at about the time men were finally deciding that there were no such things as dragons, paleontologists began to uncover the remains of the dinosaurs. Soon dinosaurs had replaced dragons in the public imagination.

In 1840 a geologist and poet named Thomas Hawkins published a book about the recently discovered extinct giant reptiles. He called his work *The Book of Great Sea Dragons*. The book was illustrated with engravings drawn with what has been described as "splendid inaccuracy." The Mesozoic monsters battled in gloomily gothic landscapes. Wrote L. Sprague de Camp: "These pictures look so much like those from medieval dragon lore that one half-expects an armored knight to clatter into the scene on his destrier." These scenes, splendidly inaccurate or not, have remained fixed in the public consciousness, and are reinforced regularly by Hollywood monster films.

So we can see that a combination of circumstances—the discovery of the fossil bones of dinosaurs at the right psychological moment, their resemblance to dragons, a general unwillingness to believe in the extinction of species, plus the genuine mysteries surrounding the death of the dinosaurs—resulted in a widespread belief that dinosaurs did remain alive out there "somewhere."

Throughout much of the nineteenth century large portions of the world's map were labeled "unexplored," which meant that they were either completely or relatively unknown to Europeans. Who knew what strange and horrible creatures might dwell somewhere in these blank areas on the map? The

steaming tropical jungles which represented a considerable
portion of the unexplored regions seemed splendid homes for
surviving dinosaurs.

Not everyone believed that there were undiscovered large
animals in the world. In 1812 Baron Georges Cuvier, the
virtual dictator of European biology, declared flatly, "There
is little hope of discovering new species of large quadrupeds."
Cuvier was also a devout believer in the theory of periodic
catastrophes and therefore an unremitting foe of all evolutionary ideas. The idea of unknown survivors from past ages
would simply not fit into his philosophy. But Cuvier's pre-
diction that all large animals were already known, was wrong,
and was proved so even in his own day.

In 1816 Cuvier learned of the "discovery" of the Indian
tapir, a large and strikingly colored animal. (Like "unexplored," the word "discovery" must be used with qualifica-
tion. The Indians and Chinese had known about the Indian
tapir for centuries. But Europeans like Cuvier had simply
refused to take the "native" accounts seriously. It was only
after a European actually shot one of the creatures that it
was officially declared to be "discovered.")

The Indian tapir was only the first of a long series of large
and unusual-looking animals to be discovered by Europeans
after 1812. It seemed that nature was full of endless surprises.
However, since the opening years of the twentieth century,
the rate of discovery has slowed considerably, and the discovery of large and unusual-looking animals has almost completely stopped. Yet the idea of dinosaurian survival was so
popular that in 1920, when the press of the world announced
that an expedition from the Smithsonian Institution was
hunting the brontosaurus—one of the largest dinosaurs that
ever existed—in Central Africa, few saw fit to question the
reality of the statement. Advice on dinosaur hunting poured
in from well-wishers throughout the world. Other hunters

set off on the trail, spurred by the rumor that the Smithsonian was offering a million pounds for the monster, dead or alive.

Surely the newspaper descriptions of the Smithsonian's brontosaurus must have caused those with even a smattering of paleontological knowledge to hesitate. The beast the expedition was hunting was described as horned and humped, while the brontosaurus, which served as the model of the Sinclair Oil dinosaur, is smooth, humpless, and hornless.

The Smithsonian did indeed have an expedition in Central Africa in 1920, but its purpose was not to hunt dinosaurs. However, expedition members had joked about the possibility of finding a dinosaur. This joke was picked up by the press and trumpeted throughout the world. Just how much of the Smithsonian dinosaur hunt story was due to exaggerations of reporters, and how much was actually due to deliberately misleading statements by members of the expedition, is not clear.

The story got so far out of hand that one of the Smithsonian's expedition members wrote a letter to the *Times* of London in which he absolutely denied that the expedition had anything to do with dinosaur hunting. He admitted that the story had started with a practical joke. The disappointing denial, of course, never received the publicity of the original sensation. So the story was widely believed, and seemed to lend a much desired stamp of official respectability to the previously dubious activity of dinosaur hunting. One may still encounter serious references to the Smithsonian's dinosaur hunt today.

In the 1930s a far cruder African dinosaur hoax made world news. J. C. Johanson, an overseer at a Belgian Congo rubber plantation, reported that he had stumbled across "a monster about sixteen yards in length, with a lizard's head and tail."

Shortly after the first encounter and still "half-paralyzed

with fear" Johanson saw the monster again. This time it was eating a dead rhinoceros. "I could plainly hear the crunching of the rhino bones in the lizard's mouth."

Johanson had a camera with him at the time and snapped a picture of the monster at its meal. This picture, if authentic, would be the most sensational in all biological history. But alas, it is only a fake and a very poor and unconvincing one at that. Johanson or someone did exactly what Hollywood has done so often, taken the picture of an ordinary lizard and superimposed it onto a background which makes it look enormous. The creature was shown perched like a clumsy ballerina atop an indistinct lump which was supposed to be the body of the rhinoceros.

But this hoax, like most hoaxes, was not made up entirely out of whole cloth, for there seems to have been some genuine Central African tradition about a huge and unknown lizardlike animal that was capable of killing prey as large as an adult rhinoceros. The legends are spread over a wide area, and are rather vague. They may have the same source or many different sources. The creature or creatures of these legends are known by a variety of names in different parts of Central Africa. But the name made famous by the Johanson hoax was *Chepekwe*.

Apparently the stories concerning the *Chepekwe* were taken quite seriously in the early years of the twentieth century by the celebrated German animal merchant Carl Hagenbeck, "The King of the Zoos," and his equally celebrated field agent Hans Schomburgk. Schomburgk was a man who made many notable animal discoveries in Central Africa, including the capture of the first pigmy hippopotamus. The opinions of these two hardheaded men, who surely knew as much about African animal life as any two Europeans alive at that time, cannot be dismissed out of hand.

Another reasonably trustworthy or at least well-known report concerns King Lewanika of Barotseland on the middle Zambezi. The king had heard rumors of the existence of a great aquatic reptile in his domain, and ordered that the next time the creature was seen he should be informed at once so that he could investigate personally.

"In the following year three men rushed into his court house one day in a great state of excitement, and said they had just seen the monster lying on the edge of the marsh, and that on viewing them it had retreated on its belly, and slid into the deep water. The beast was said to be of colossal size, with legs like a gigantic lizard, and possessing a long neck. It was said to be taller than a man, and had a head like a snake.

"Lewanika at once rode to the spot and saw a large space where the reeds had been flattened down, and a broad path with water flowing into the recently disturbed mud, made to the water's edge. He described the channel made by the body of the supposed monsters to Colonel Hardinge, the British Resident, 'as large as a full-sized wagon from which the wheels had been removed.'"

The testimony of Hagenbeck, Schomburgk, and King Lewanika is generally considered the most persuasive evidence for the existence of some sort of dinosaurlike reptile in the middle of Africa. Such testimony, however, despite the reliability and experience of the witnesses, is of little real value. The three men have merely expressed a belief in the existence of such a creature. They have not come forth with evidence that the thing actually does exist. They do not, for example, provide us with eyewitness accounts of the beast in action.

The eyewitness accounts are either highly dubious, like that of J. C. Johanson, or very vague or in other ways thoroughly unsatisfactory. In any case, they are not very numerous. The native traditions which are so often called upon as support for the idea of a living African dinosaur are also vague and could easily stem from highly colored descriptions of a number of different but well-known animals.

As it turned out, the more closely Central Africa was explored the less was heard of the African dinosaur. Dinosaur stories just about stopped coming out of Africa after the 1930s.

In 1950, however, a reported encounter with a dinosaur reminiscent of those which came from Africa in the early years of the century was published in England. This dinosaur-like monster was found in the jungles of the island of New Guinea. The reputed discoverer was Charles "Cannibal" Miller, an English adventurer and would-be explorer.

Miller's account was quite melodramatic, and the monster itself was described as having a suspicious mixture of characteristics: long neck and tail, horns, crest, and armored plates. This dinosaur sounded so much like a virtual encyclopedia of half-digested paleontology that one immediately suspects that the story was never meant to be taken seriously in the first place.

Yet, Miller claimed that he had photographs and a piece of horn from the New Guinea monster. Needless to say, neither horn nor photographs has ever been put on public display. "Cannibal" Miller's encounter with the dinosaur must be ranked as a prime modern example of the traveler's tale.

When you come right down to it, the case for the current survival of the dinosaur is very weak. But let us consider another possibility. Although the dinosaur may be extinct today, some of them did live on until relatively recent times, and somehow got embedded into mankind's mythology. We have already discussed this possibility in the relationship of dinosaurs to the dragon of Europe and the Orient. This was rejected simply because no dinosaurs were really needed to explain the origins of most dragon myths. But the case of the *sirrush* or Babylonian dragon is a bit different.

Sometime during his reign (605–562 B.C.) King Nebuchadnezzar of Babylon rebuilt the great Ishtar Gate which spanned one of the roads leading into the city of Babylon. The gate, like most Babylonian structures, was made from baked brick and faced with colored, glazed brick. For decoration the gate was adorned with rows of reliefs of animals. Two creatures dominate the decorations. One is referred to in the Babylonian inscriptions as the *rimi*. The *rimi* is shown as a large bull-like animal. It has been identified as the aurochs, the now extinct ancestor of our domestic cattle. The other creature on the Ishtar gate was the *sirrush,* a word which we have often translated as "dragon." (Another translation of this creature's name has been given as "glamour snake." It seems wise to stick with dragon.)

This "dragon" of the Ishtar Gate does not fit the conventional picture of the Western or Oriental dragon. The body is scaly and reptilian, all right, but the tail is not nearly so long or thick as that of the more familiar dragons. The thick neck is long and topped by a small head. The head is adorned by what appears to be a single straight horn above the eye, and a number of rather incongruous curlicues. A forked tongue protrudes from the creature's mouth. But the strangest and most significant features of the *sirrush* are its legs. These are long and quite unlike the legs of any other dragon. The Babylonian dragon's hind legs end in great birdlike claws, while the front legs resemble those of a lion or some other large cat.

The people of Mesopotamia, as we have noted, were masters at creating fabulous animals, and the *sirrush* might easily nother of these imaginary conglomerations, no more real man-headed bulls or winged lions of the Assyrians.

But not everybody has regarded the *sirrush* as an undoubtedly mythical animal.

The first man to put forth the possibility that the dragon of the Ishtar Gate was based on a living model was one of the first men in modern times to gaze upon it, Professor Robert Koldeway, who in 1920 directed the expeditions which led to the excavation of the Ishtar Gate.

Koldeway was, of course, not unaware of the reconstructions of dinosaurs that other scientists were making. To him the *sirrush* resembled the extinct dinosaurs in some really extraordinary ways. "If only the forelegs were not so emphatically and characteristically feline, such an animal might actually have existed," Koldeway wrote in 1913.

Five years later he had still been unable to give up the idea that the *sirrush* was or had been a real animal. In a publication about the Ishtar Gate he wrote, "The *Iguanodon* of the Cretaceous layers of Belgium is the closest relative of the Dragon of Babylon."

The key features that led Koldeway to his identification of the *sirrush* with the *Iguanodon* were the birdlike hind feet and the horns. Besides, the *Iguanodon* was simply the best-known dinosaur of the time. With today's greater knowledge others have suggested that the dragon of the Ishtar Gate more closely resembles the carnivorous *Ceratosaurus* than the plant-eating *Iguanodon*.

But whatever dinosaur one wishes to relate the *sirrush* to, the resemblance is not all that close. The great birdlike hind feet do seem to be typical of those dinosaurs which walked upright on their hind feet, and used their small and degenerate front feet for grasping and tearing only. (In medieval times artists put birdlike feet on some of their dragons.) But we again confront the problem of the catlike front feet which seem not only the wrong shape, but much too large for a bird-footed dinosaur.

According to tradition the Babylonians actually kept a dragon which they worshipped as a god. Daniel killed the Babylonian dragon by giving it a pill made of bitumen and hair. But if the Babylonians really did keep some sort of surviving dinosaur, Nebuchadnezzar's artists copied it with almost astonishing inaccuracy. A dinosaur with the back feet of a bird and the front feet of a lion is a biological impossibility.

The late Willy Ley suggested that perhaps the reason for the curious dinosaurlike, yet undinosaurlike characteristics of the *sirrush*, was that, despite the tale of Daniel, the *sirrush* was not seen in Babylon. Rather, Ley suggested, the *sirrush* was a creature that dwelt in a far-off land and was known to the Babylonians only through traveler's tales, hence the inaccuracy of the representation of it on the Ishtar Gate.

Ley made a telling point—the aurochs which served as the model for the bull reliefs of the Ishtar Gate was also represented very inaccurately, probably because the Babylonian artists had never seen one. The aurochs had once lived in Mesopotamia, but was probably extinct there long before the time of Nebuchadnezzar. The aurochs still lived on in the distant forests of Europe, but in Mesopotamia itself it was known only through stories and ancient drawings. Might not the same be true of the model for the *sirrush?* But what distant land might be the home of this surviving dinosaur?

Ley pointed out that before Koldeway published most of his speculations on the *sirrush* and the dinosaur, our old acquaintance Hans Schomburgk, the animal collector who had believed in the possibility of surviving dinosaurs in Africa, had brought back from Central Africa some glazed brick, similar to that used as facing on the Ishtar Gate. Here we have a connection, admittedly a tenuous one, but still a connection, between the Central African home of the most persistent of the surviving dinosaur stories and the curious dragon of the Ishtar Gate.

The scientific community did not react to Ley's ingenious theory with much enthusiasm. Edwin H. Colbert charged that the theory "digs up all the old specious arguments on whether dinosaurs still exist, and hashes them over again." Colbert's argument against the *sirrush* was simple and impressive: not a single scrap of material proof of dinosaurian survival beyond the Cretaceous period has ever been found.

"Negative evidence only," grumble the monster buffs, when confronted with such arguments. Yet one wonders what other sort of evidence there could be for the nonexistence of a creature.

The dinosaurs are not the only great beasts of the past who have been nominated as candidates for survival. Around the end of the Pleistocene period or Ice Age, a mere ten thousand years ago, large numbers of gigantic mammals marched ingloriously to extinction. The number of gigantic mammals that exist or have existed into historical times, particuarly in North and South America and Europe, represent only a pitiful remnant of the enormous number of giants that once lived on these continents.

The problem of the Pleistocene extinctions is even more puzzling than that of the extinction of the dinosaurs. After all, ten thousand years is a mere blink of the eye when compared to the seventy million years since the death of the dinosaurs. Knowledge of the factors which may have accounted for the extinction of the dinosaurs could simply have been lost to us by the passing of so many millions of years. We know a great deal more about the conditions of the earth ten thousand years ago. We know, for example, that from a geological point of view, the earth was essentially the same as it is today. (The repeated advance and retreat of the glaciers is not considered a major geological change.) There was no obvious reason for the mass extinction of large animals.

The subject of the Pleistocene extinctions is a newly awakened area of interest among scientists. The debates they have conducted over the puzzle are long and complex. They need not concern us here. A single example will suffice to show just how puzzling the problem is.

The horse evolved in North America. The rocks contain as clear and complete a record of the evolution of the horse as we have for any other creature. But then at the end of the Pleistocene the horse disappeared from North America. However, horses survived in Asia, where they were ultimately domesticated and finally brought back to North America by the Spanish conquistadors. Some of the Spaniards' horses escaped and went wild. They flourished in their ancestral environment, and for a time wild horses again became a fixed part of the North American fauna.

The horse's habitat obviously had not disappeared when the horse did. Why then did the horse die out in the first place? That in a nutshell is the problem posed by the Pleistocene extinctions. Large animals died out when there seemed no reason for them to have died out. And if there was no reason for them to have died out might not some of them have survived?

No one has bothered much about the possibility that horses had survived in North America between the end of the Pleistocene and the coming of the Spanish. The elephant is another matter. It is quite large enough and might be terrifying enough to quite properly be classed as a monster. There has been plenty of speculation and even some passionate arguments over whether elephants of one sort or another have survived in places where they are generally thought not to have existed since the Ice Age ended.

Today elephants are still reasonably numerous in parts of

Asia and Africa, but there remain only two closely related genera whose range is limited to tropical portions of the Old World. During the Pleistocene at least a half dozen vastly different kinds of elephants and their near relatives roamed both hemispheres from the equator to the edge of the ice sheets. The two presumably extinct forms of elephant that are of most interest to us are the mammoths and the mastodons.

In the early years of the nineteenth century the idea that man and the now extinct varieties of elephants could have existed at the same time seemed unthinkable to many. That was the era of catastrophic theories and the mammoths and mastodons, whose bones were found in such abundance, were thought to be creatures that lived in the age before the Universal Deluge or some other world-wide catastrophe. They were creatures that had been wiped from the face of the earth before the creation of man. The discovery that mammoths were favorite subjects of cave painters came as a rather rude shock. Soon artifacts of man in association with the remains of extinct elephants, for example, an arrowhead embedded between the ribs of a mammoth skeleton, began to turn up rather frequently.

Ironically, the first discovery of an association between man and extinct giant animals in North America seems to have been made by "Dr." Albert Koch, the notorious fabricator of fossil monsters. In addition to his mountebank personality, Koch really was a skilled excavator of fossils. In 1838 he discovered arrowheads along with what seemed to be the charred bones of a mastodon. (From his description, it appears today that the bones may actually have been those of the equally extinct giant ground sloth. The point here is that this is the first reported find associating an extinct animal with man in North America.)

Unfortunately by the time Koch published a description

of his find, his flamboyant fossil reconstructions and other exaggerated claims had so damaged his reputation that most scientists refused to take the report seriously. It was not until nearly a century later that the association of man and extinct animals in North America was definitely established. The evidence that man in America once hunted mammoth, giant ground sloth and long-horned buffalo, is now so abundant that many scientists seriously believe that it was the hunters who brought about the extinction of these creatures.

We are on firm ground if we say that the American mastodon and at least two varieties of mammoth, the imperial and the woolly, existed in huge numbers throughout the Western hemisphere, and that these creatures were both seen and hunted by the direct ancestors of today's American Indians. But when did the elephants die out? And did the Indians remember the elephants up until the time of the coming of the white man?

There are some North American Indian legends which seem to speak of monsters with decidely elephantlike appearances. These legends might have been inspired by mammoths or mastodons surviving well beyond the Pleistocene, or they may have been part of a really ancient tradition dating back thousands of years to Pleistocene times. But neither explanation is really necessary. These "elephant legends" are not numerous and not very clear. It is entirely possible that they do not in any way relate to elephants—ancient or recent. This is the view held by the majority of zoologists.

The story of an English seaman who in 1580 walked from the Gulf of Mexico to Nova Scotia and along the way reported seeing herds of "huge, shaggy creatures with long trunks" is also highly suspect.

The reputed elephant artifacts give us something a bit more substantial to work with. The most famous, and certainly the largest of these, is the so-called Elephant Mound of Wisconsin. Throughout the Mississippi Valley and the southeastern United States the Indians of past ages built huge ceremonial burial mounds. Many of these mounds were made to resemble various birds and animals. If the Wisconsin mound was meant to resemble an elephant, then the case for the survival of North American elephants well beyond Pleistocene times would be immeasurably strengthened, for the mounds of America are not more than a thousand years old. But that's the rub: Is the mound meant to resemble an elephant? The mound displays neither tusks, tail, nor large ears, all prominent features of elephants. The trunk itself seems too stiff and short for an elephant, even a highly stylized elephant.

Critics of the elephant theory claim that the "elephant mound" is in reality a bear mound to which flooding or some other accident of nature added a trunklike extension at the front end. Bears were common subjects for effigy mounds.

Although one may reasonably doubt that the elephant mound shows an elephant, the elephants on the elephant pipes are undoubted likenesses. The Indians who built the mounds also made pipes which were topped with the figures of animals. In 1878 and again in 1880, pipes containing what certainly looked like figures of elephants were found in the vicinity of Davenport, Iowa. The instigator of both finds was the Reverend Jacob Gass, a Lutheran clergyman of Davenport. The Reverend Mr. Gass had already made many remarkable and unexpected discoveries in the Davenport mounds. A little too remarkable and unexpected, in the opinion of his many critics. Among other things he found in the mounds were inscribed tablets containing Roman, Arabic, Phoenician and Hebrew characters. Yet another of these tablets had the twelve signs of the zodiac. At the time many believed the mounds to be the relics of a great vanished and presumably white civilization that had once lived in North

America. The Reverend Mr. Gass was an ardent supporter of such theories.

Scientists from the Smithsonian Institution soon struck out at the "elephant pipes" and came very close to publicly accusing the clergyman of actually fabricating the relics himself. No definite proof of fraud has ever been put forward, but the more that was discovered about the mounds the more wildly out of line with reality the elephant pipes and other discoveries of Jacob Gass seemed. Today, the most polite thing that can be said of the items from the Davenport mounds is that they are highly suspect.

Something else which troubled scientists concerning the coexistence of mound builders and mastodon was that while the remains of many animals were found buried within the mounds, there was not a single scrap of ivory or other identifiable remains from any member of the elephant clan. A possible reason for this is that by the time the mound builders were around, the mastodon had gone a long way down the road to extinction and was exceedingly rare. A more probable reason is that there were no mastodons at all.

Another artifact that is even more suspect than the elephant pipes is the Lenape stone which was found on a farm in Bucks County, Pennsylvania, in 1872. The stone shows a crude but clear picture of Indians hunting a woolly mammoth. More than anything else, the stone looks like a rather amateurish attempt to copy the cave paintings of Europe, and this is exactly what most experts believe it to be.

Elephants also lived in Central and South America in Pleistocene times. The best paleontological evidence available indicates that these elephants too became extinct about ten thousand years ago—certainly well before the rise of the Mayas, Incas, and other great Indian civilizations of pre-Columbian America. Yet the most celebrated piece of evidence for the late survival of elephants in America is the so-called elephant stela at the Mayan city of Tikal.

Carved in relief on this large slab of stone are what appears, at first glance, to be the representation of a pair of elephant heads. Each elephant is topped by a Mayan mahout riding on the elephant's neck. But Mayan art is highly stylized rather than realistic and the skeptics have pointed to some odd features of these Tikal "elephants." For example, they have nostrils at the base of their trunks, rather than at the tip, where they should be. They also possess what appear to be feathers. These "elephants," say the skeptics, are in reality conventionalized birds—macaws—whose hooked beaks have been mistaken for elephants trunks by enthusiasts.

Some early explorers returned from South and Central American ruins with numerous drawings of what appeared to be elephants, copied from Indian carvings. Later investigation proved that virtually all these "elephant" drawings had been the result of inaccurate copying. The explorers had been looking for elephants, and they were able to find "elephants" in the unfamiliar and intricate carvings of the pre-Columbian Indians. Many of these carvings were badly weathered, or mutilated, so the copyists tried to "reconstruct" them as they had originally appeared.

The long and eager search to find evidence of elephants in the Americas does not stem merely from the romantic notion that mammoths and mastodons survived into fairly recent times. It drew its principal inspiration from the diffusionist theory of culture. The diffusionists hold that all cultures started in a single place, or at the most a very few places. From there they spread by migration throughout the entire world. The chief aim of the diffusionists has been to prove that the Indian civilizations of the Western Hemisphere have their roots in the civilizations of Asia.

Diffusionism is a perfectly respectable philosophy, although it is not much in favor today. But on the far shores of diffusionism are many individuals who hold genuinely bizarre ideas. Chief among these fringe diffusionists, are the Atlantists, who believe that all human culture had its beginning on the now sunken island continent of Atlantis that once existed in the middle of the Atlantic Ocean.

The number one theoretician and leading light of the Atlantists was Ignatius Donnelly, rightly titled "America's Prince of Cranks." Donnelly's work on Atlantis, which links practically everything under the sun to the lost island continent, is still the bible of the Atlantists today although it was first published way back in 1882. For ingenuity, persistence, and just plain wrongheadedness, Donnelly has never been surpassed, and probably never will be.

Wrote Donnelly: "We find in America numerous representations of the elephant. We are forced to one of two conclusions: Either the monuments date back to the time of the mammoth in North America, or these people did intercourse at some time in the past with races who possessed the elephant, and from whom they obtained pictures of that singular animal. Plato tells us that Atlanteans possessed great numbers of elephants.

"There are in Wisconsin a number of mounds of earth representing different animals—men, birds, and quadrupeds. Among the latter is a mound representing an elephant, 'so perfect in its proportions, and complete in its representation of an elephant, that its builders must have been well acquainted with all the physical characteristics of the animal which they delineated.'

"On a farm in Louisa County, Iowa, a pipe was plowed up which also represents an elephant. It was found in a section where the ancient mounds were very abundant and rich in relics. The pipe is of sandstone, of the ordinary Mound Builder's type, and has every appearance of age and usage. There can be no doubt of its genuineness."

From the above quote it should be obvious that Donnelly was quite willing to overlook any objections that got in the way of his pet theory. He had grossly overstated the case for the elephant in America, but his theories were influential and still are for Atlantists, who continue to look for and find pictures of elephants in the Americas.

Donnelly had his Atlanteans escaping from the destruction of their homeland and reaching South America. Thereafter they discovered the mouth of the Mississippi River and explored all its tributaries. Throughout these wanderings they carried with them the memory of the elephants of their homeland.

Others have theorized that there are drawings and other representations of elephants in the Americas because the American Indians came from Asia and carried with them the "idea of the elephant." The American Indians did indeed migrate from Asia across the dry Bering Strait. These early Indians were almost certainly skilled in elephant hunting, for they would have hunted elephants throughout Siberia. One of the reasons they migrated may well have been because of the abundance of elephants in the Americas. But the earliest Americans were not, as far as we know, artists, and left no representations of their huge prey. There is simply no good evidence that later Indians had retained any "idea of the elephant" or had encountered any living elephants to draw or sculpt. One should not be dogmatic on this point. It is not impossible, perhaps not even improbable, that some sort of undoubted Indian representations of elephants will someday turn up in the Americas. But so far they have not.

Of all the now extinct elephants, the one that is popularly considered to be the best candidate for late survival is the woolly mammoth. As its name implies, this creature was a cold-weather animal. It often lived on the very fringes of the glaciers. As a result the frozen remains of the woolly mammoth have occasionally been found in a remarkable state of preservation. This has led to the belief that these remains of woolly mammoths are of a more recent date than the less well-preserved remains of the American mastodon, the imperial mammoth, or other Pleistocene elephants. In fact, mastodon bones have been radiocarbon dated at a mere six to eight thousand years old, making them several thousand years more recent than the most recent of the dated woolly mammoth remains. The best known of the frozen mammoth carcasses has been dated at twenty-five thousand years. (These mastodon dates are, however, somewhat suspect, for the remains may have been contaminated, thus rendering the dates inaccurate.)

Stories that mammoths were still alive and well in Alaska during the last century got started in a rather unusual way. During the 1890s a naturalist from the United States Fish Commission bought some mammoth ivory from Eskimos at Cape Prince of Wales. The Eskimos had no idea what sort of animal the ivory had come from, so the obliging naturalist showed them a picture of a reconstruction of a woolly mammoth in a book that he happened to have with him. The Eskimos were fascinated by the picture of this strange-looking beast, and they made a sketch of it to show their friends.

You can guess what happened after that. As the sketch was passed from hand to hand and recopied many times, its origin was forgotten. Instead of being a drawing that had been copied from a book, it soon became a drawing made from firsthand observation of the mighty beast tromping through the Alaskan tundra. After a while word of the Alaskan mammoth reached the white trappers and traders. They were skeptical at first. But they wondered how the Eskimos could know about mammoths if they hadn't actually seen one. Finally, many of the white men became convinced that such a creature really did still exist in Alaska.

From the traders the story of the mammoth was passed southward, and paragraphs about it began to appear not only in the press of Alaska but in parts of the United States as well. The story reached its apex of foolishness in October 1899, when *McClure's Magazine* published an article by a man named Henry Tukeman. The author claimed to have shot the last surviving mammoth in Alaska. The tale was complete with descriptions of the great beast's death throes. To crown the story, the author said the mammoth's hide and bones had been purchased for the Smithsonian Institution.

The story was a hoax, and the annual index of the *McClure's Magazine* dutifully lists "The Killing of the Mammoth" as fiction. But there was no indication in the pages of the issue in which the story appeared that it was anything other than a factual account, so many people took it seriously. Visitors to the Smithsonian often demanded to see the mammoth remains, which they believed were, for some obscure reason, being kept hidden from the public. Elaborate assurances that no such remains existed were often not believed, and many visitors left feeling that they had been cheated, not by the magazine, but by the Smithsonian Institution.

In Siberia the remains of the mammoth are so common that the tusks of these long-dead elephants once formed an important item of trade. During the closing years of the nineteenth century some fifty thousand pounds of mammoth ivory was being sold every year in the market at Yakutsk. This weight of ivory must have represented the remains of at least two hundred individual mammoths. It has been estimated that over the centuries the remains of as many as one hundred thousand mammoths have been uncovered in one state of preservation or another throughout Siberia.

The presence of these huge bones in such great numbers, as well as the occasional find of a well-preserved frozen carcass, had to be explained somehow. The mammoth remains led to a large number of legends about huge beasts that either had lived or still were living underground in Siberia. The name mammoth itself may originally have come from a Turkish word that means "mole." The Tatars also believed that the mammoths were really monsters that inhabited the interior of the earth but died immediately upon seeing the light of the sun. This explained why, although there were plenty of dead mammoths, no one had ever seen a living mammoth. (Belief in the underground mammoth is quite reminiscent of the European belief that dragons were underground creatures.)

Another possible derivation of the word mammoth is that it was the result of a long series of mispronunciations of behemoth, the name of that rather ill-defined monster of the Bible. The Russians often identified the remains of the mammoth as those of the behemoth simply because they did not know what else to call them.

When the people of Siberia got around to attempting to reconstruct a picture of the living animal from the mammoth remains that they found, they came up with a variety of creatures. None of them looked like elephants. Even the partially preserved carcasses inspired description of unicorns or other decidedly un-elephantlike beasts. The first people to recognize that the mammoth remains had come from elephants were outsiders who already knew what elephants looked like, and thus could recognize them from fragmentary remains.

The ancestors of the Siberians had hunted mammoths in such great numbers that they had been able to construct homes from their bones. But the modern Siberians had lost all knowledge of living mammoths' appearance. When they came upon a frozen mammoth they regarded it with superstitious terror. Therefore, it seems quite clear that no one in Siberia had seen a living mammoth for many millennia—or had they?

In 1918 an old Russian hunter is reported to have told the French consul at Vladivostok that he had tracked a "huge elephant with big white tucks, very curved; it was a dark chestnut colour as far as I could see. It had fairly long hair on the hind quarters but it seemed shorter on the front."

Another story concerns the Don Cossack Yermak Timofeyevitch who in 1580 saw "a large hairy elephant" in Siberia. These elephants were supposed to be well known to the natives of a certain part of Siberia. They were frequently hunted, and were referred to as "the mountain of meat."

The Siberian tundra is very remote from the centers of civilization. It is thinly populated, and outsiders do not venture onto it regularly. Yet it is virtually impossible to imagine that a herd of large hairy elephants could live there and not be reported rather frequently. Yet two reports three hundred and thirty-eight years apart are all the evidence that we have for the survival of the woolly mammoth in Siberia.

The tundra is open and, unlike the jungle, there is no place for elephants to hide. But Bernard Heuvelmans has speculated that, contrary to popular opinion, the woolly mammoth was not really a creature of the tundra. The woolly mammoth, says Heuvelmans, was more likely to live in the taiga, the vast belt of northern forest that stretches across Soviet Asia. The taiga is the largest forest in the world, and the most unexplored. Since it is bitterly cold in the winter, boggy and insect-infested in the summer, people do not like to go into it. Is it possible for elephants to hide within this dismal area and go unnoticed for centuries? Says Heuvelmans, "Herds of hundreds or even thousands of mammoths could easily live there without running the least risk of being seen by man." Few zoologists, or geographers for that matter, would agree with Heuvelmans on that point, but it is something to think about.

While the remains of recently dead mammoths might easily become confused with the abundant remains of long-dead mammoths, and thus go unidentified, the lack of any substantial tradition of living mammoths is perhaps the greatest single obstacle in the way of believing that the woolly mammoth, that monster of the Ice Age, still survives.

There is somewhat better evidence for the survival of another monster from the past. Picture for a moment an animal as big as an ox, but capable of standing on its hind legs. The creature's front feet are tipped with enormous sickle-like claws that are used for digging the burrows in which it spends most of its days. Add the detail that the creature is almost impervious to arrows or bullets and you have a description of a monster that forms part of the folklore of the Indians of Patagonia and Argentina. But you also have a pretty good description of a real animal that once lived in that area—the giant ground sloth.

Like so many other huge mammals, the giant ground sloth (or rather a whole tribe of ground sloths ranging from the elephant-sized *Megatherium* to creatures just a few feet tall) was supposed to have died out some ten thousand years ago. But a number of intriguing hints from Patagonia indicate that the giant sloth may have survived well beyond that date, indeed that it may still survive even today.

Besides the Indian traditions, there is the story of Ramón Lista, an Argentine politician, geographer, and explorer. In the 1890s Lista reported that he and his companions saw what looked like a large, hairy armadillo in Patagonia. Lista tried to shoot the creature in order to study it more closely, but the bullets did not seem to have any effect and it escaped.

A third hint comes from a piece of hide that was hung on a fence in an isolated ranch in Patagonia. The hide, which was covered with brown hair and which seemed fairly fresh, was studded with little bones. It was almost certainly a piece of hide from a medium-sized ground sloth known as *Mylodon*.

In 1898 these three bits of evidence were weighed by Professor Florentino Ameghino, Argentina's number one fossil hunter. He came to the conclusion that the ground sloth was alive and well in Patagonia. He gave the creature the name *Neomylodon listai* in honor of Lista who had recently been killed. Most scientists, however, would not accept Professor Ameghino's conclusions. During his career Ameghino had made many notable discoveries, but he had also made many notable blunders. His enthusiasm too often led him wildly astray, and the bulk of the scientific community frankly distrusted his judgment.

The Indian legends could be discounted as misinterpretations. Even Ameghino himself had at first disbelieved Lista's account. But the piece of *Mylodon* hide, that was something else again. Bits of it had been examined by many scientists and there seemed no doubt that it was a piece of fresh hide that belonged to a presumably extinct animal.

The hide was ultimately traced to a ranch in far southern Argentina near the dismally titled Last Hope Inlet. The rancher, a German immigrant named Eberhardt, discovered the skin in a nearby cave in 1895.

Repeated expeditions to Eberhardt's cave brought forth some fairly spectacular finds, including evidence that man, as well as *Mylodon*, had lived in the cave. One of the explorers, Dr. Rudolph Hauthal, believed that he had found evidence that domesticated giant sloths had actually been kept in the cave. Today most authorities believe that Dr. Hauthal's conclusions were based on erroneous interpretations of the evidence, but they created a mild sensation when first advanced. The theory of the domesticated sloth even produced a new, albeit short-lived name for the beast, *Grypotherium domesticum,* "the domesticated griffin mammal."

In recent years scientists have been able to radiocarbon date some of the material from the cave. Nothing tested gives the slightest hint that the *Mylodon* lived there beyond ten thousand years ago and thus well within the conventional time boundary set for the beast's extinction. The apparent freshness of the *Mylodon* hide found in the cave remains difficult to account for. Still, rodent skins and other biological specimens, in a remarkably good state of preservation, have been taken from the cave. The *Mylodon* skin itself was apparently found deep within the cave where it was more likely to have been well preserved, than at the mouth of the cave, where it was originally reported to have been found.

So it seems that the piece of bone-studded hide, which looked like conclusive proof that the old legends were true, turns out to be less than conclusive after all. Well over half a century has passed since it was discovered, and nothing at all has been added to the tale of the giant sloth of Patagonia. In theory the survival of such a monster until modern times is not impossible, not even unlikely. But that a beast as large and unusual-looking as a ground sloth could escape conclusive detection for well over half a century is unlikely indeed.

Numerous other large animals, supposedly extinct since the Pleistocene or before, have from time to time been advanced as possible candidates for survival. However, the evidence for such survival is usually no more than a casual resemblance between the creature and a monster described in some legend. Occasionally, however, we have a bit more than legendary evidence. A notable example is the case of the Sumerian "stag."

At Kish in Iraq archaeologists dug up a small copper rein

ring. It was part of the harness equipment used on chariots by the Sumerians around 3500 B.C. Usually such objects were decorated with the small figure of a horse, but this particular one bore the figure of a stocky horned animal. Archaeologists labeled the figure that of a stag.

In 1936, however, Dr. Edwin H. Colbert (the man who, you will recall, had so ferociously spiked any thought of dinosaurian survival) decided that the figure looked more like *Sivatherium* than a stag. *Sivatherium* is, or rather was, a relative of the giraffe. Paleontologists believe that it has been extinct for many thousands of years.

Did this large and singular-looking creature survive several millennia beyond its supposed extinction? Was it known to the Sumerians? And, even more surprising, was it domesticated by the Sumerians? The presence of a rope from the muzzle of the little bronze figure suggests that the creature that served as model for it was not a wild animal.

The little figure is a reminder that not only prehistoric hunters, but also some of the early civilizations as well may have been acquainted with creatures that are today known only as fossils. Some of these creatures may have become incorporated in legends and stories, and these once-living animals may well have been passed on to us as monsters.

Monsters from Space

The year 1952 marked one of the periodic high points in America's longtime fascination with the possibility that the earth was being visited by saucer-shaped vehicles from outer space. On the evening of September 12 some boys in the small town of Flatwoods (population 300) in Braxton County, West Virginia, spotted a red glowing "something" traveling through the sky. Whatever it was appeared to land or crash just beyond the crest of a nearby hill, and the boys decided to investigate.

On their way to the hill they passed a house occupied by the May family. Mrs. Kathleen May, a beautician in a nearby town, came out to ask them where they were going. " A flying saucer has landed on the hill and we're going to look at it," one of the boys replied. Mrs. May, her two young sons, and a teen-age neighbor joined the search, and another youngster was added to the party somewhere along the way. The seven hurried up the hill getting more excited all the time.

To get to the spot of the landing they had to open a high
fence gate. Before going on they carefully closed the gate
behind them. A dog belonging to one of the boys had come
along with the group and it streaked ahead toward the area
of the "landing" barking furiously. A few seconds later they
saw the dog streaking silently in the other direction, with its
tail between its legs. As the seven rounded the last bend in
the trail toward the landing spot they saw an eerie light and
were assailed by a sickening smell, so powerful that it caused
their eyes to water and produced attacks of vomiting for
hours afterwards.

Then they saw "it." Just what "it" was has been a matter of
some dispute since.

The United Press quoted Mrs. May as saying they had seen
"a fire-breathing monster, ten feet tall with a bright green
body and blood-red face" and it waddled toward them with
"a bouncing floating" motion. She added, "It looked worse
than Frankenstein. It couldn't have been human."

Gray Barker, a West Virginia flying saucer enthusiast and
publisher of flying saucer books, came rushing to the scene
at the request of *Fate* Magazine. Barker interviewed the witnesses and produced this description:

"Fifteen feet away, towering over their heads, was a vast
shape something like a man. The face, everyone agreed, was
round, and blood red. No one noticed a nose or mouth, only
eyes, or eye-like openings from which projected 'greenish
orange' beams of light ... Around the red 'face' and reaching
upward to a point was a dark, hood-like shape. The body was
seen only from the 'head' down to the 'waist.' It appeared
dark and colorless [to one of the boys] though some said it
was green ... Mrs. May said it lighted up when the flashlight
beam touched it as if there were some source of illumination
inside it. She also saw clothing-like folds around the body,

and terrible claws. No one was sure whether the shape rested on the ground or was floating."

Old monster-hand Ivan Sanderson came to Flatwoods at the urging of "a leading national magazine" and the North American Newspaper Alliance. After interviewing the witnesses he came up with this composite description:

"The entity's top was level with a branch of the tree, and seemed to end about some six feet below. It was about the size of an enormous man down to the waist. It did not have any arms or anything else sticking out of it, but it had a distinct 'head.' This was shaped like an 'ace of spades' . . . However, this 'head' had a large circular window in it through which they could see (a) darkness and (b) two 'things like eyes, which stayed fixed and shone straight out.' "

There are, as you can see, some fairly important differences between these three accounts. This is hardly surprising considering the acknowledged state of the seven witnesses after viewing the "monster." One of the boys "passed out" and had to be hauled to his feet by the others. As the monster seemed to be advancing toward the party everyone ran. One of the boys recalls seeing Mrs. May clear the closed six-foot gate in one fantastic leap. Back at the May house they found the dog had already beaten them home and was cowering on the porch.

A party of gun-toting adults quickly gathered and headed for the hill where the monster had been seen. They found nothing and returned openly skeptical that anything unusual had happened. Word continued to spread and within two hours the sheriff was at the May house. Reporters for local papers followed quickly.

An investigation of the "landing site" the next day was disappointing. The searchers could find no material evidence except for some unexplained flattened areas in the grass. The local police declared that the seven who had seen the "mon-

ster" were victims of "mass hysteria," and declined further
investigation. Cooler heads in the community theorized that
this is what happened:

The boys had seen a bright meteor apparently crash behind the hill. Others in neighboring areas had also reported
seeing a meteor, although no trace of its hitting the ground
was found. This, however, is not unusual, for most meteors
burn up before striking the earth. The group was in a highly
excited state even before they reached the hilltop. Remember, there was only one adult among the witnesses. Another
witness was seventeen (that was the boy who fainted) and
all the others were under fourteen. At the landing site, or
what they took to be the landing site, they saw a pair of
glowing eyes staring at them. Perhaps what they really saw
was eyeshine from a raccoon or opossum sitting up in a tree.
The darkness, a bit of mountain fog, and youthful imagina-
tions fed by several years of sensational reports of "flying
saucers" did the rest.

By all rights the story of the Flatwoods' monster should
have ended right there. But it did not. It continued to grow
for several weeks. The wire services picked up the story, and
it was published in newspapers throughout the country. Mrs.
May and the oldest of the boys went to New York for radio
and television interviews. Magazines offered farfetched explanations of what the Flatwoods' monster might be. Most
of the stories were skeptical, if not downright cynical about
what had happened on the hilltop near Flatwoods. But the
old advertising axiom "I don't care what you say about me
so long as you spell my name right" was at work for the Flatwoods monster. The more people who heard about the monster, even if they only heard jokes about it, the more people
there were who believed that there was "something" to the
story.

Incredibly, this painfully thin story made a listing of the

ten biggest feature stories of the year. The Flatwoods monster was even dubbed a "land-locked Loch Ness Monster."

If the initial account had been followed up by other sightings, the result might well have been a vigorous addition to current monster lore. But after the first sighting nothing at all happened. Years afterwards those who had been involved in the original incident seemed reluctant to discuss it any further. Flying saucer buffs hint rather broadly that they have been "silenced" by the government or by somebody or something even more sinister.

The Flatwoods monster has now become part of the established mythology of what might be called the occult underground. The occult underground is a large but loose conglomeration of organizations and individuals who share common beliefs and interests in bizarre or fringe subjects. This could include anything from flying saucers to astrology, from communicating with the dead to hollow-earth theories to a number of offbeat varieties of Christianity. This group has become so large today it might be called the occult subculture.

I have quite recently heard the Flatwoods monster described in a lecture which also discussed the meaning of flying saucers in relation to the Bible. Although I have never heard this particular monster identified with the beast of Revelation, I would not be at all surprised if such an identification had not been made at some meeting or in some publication of the occult underground.

The Flatwoods monster attained another sort of immortality. It became the subject of a country and western ballad. The ballad called "The Phantom of Flatwoods" is sung to the tune of "Sweet Betsy from Pike" and one of the verses goes:

> The size of the phantom was a sight to behold
> Green eyes and red face, so the story was told.

It floated in air with fingers of flame.
It was gone with a hiss, just as quick as it came.

And the chorus runs:

Oh, Phantom of Flatwoods, from Moon or from Mars
Maybe from God and not from the stars,
Please tell us why you fly o'er our trees.
The end of the world or an omen of peace?

Fourteen years after the Flatwoods monster appeared and then disappeared "just as quick as it came" another monster from outer space showed up in West Virginia and many memories of Flatwoods were revived.

Actually it is a little difficult to determine just exactly why this second West Virginia monster became known as a monster from space. Although the Flatwoods monster was connected directly with the supposed landing of a flying saucer, this second monster was not. However, it was sighted in the area of Point Pleasant, West Virginia, and strange lights had been reported in the sky at about the same time. In addition, 1966 was a time of heightened interest in flying saucers or UFOs. John Fuller's *The Interrupted Journey,* a best seller about a New England couple who claimed to have been kidnapped by spacemen, was much talked about. But perhaps the most important reason that the Point Pleasant monster became known as a monster from space was because those who were most deeply involved in investigating and publicizing it were men like Gray Barker, who were already luminaries in the field of "saucer investigation."

The story started late on the evening of November 15, 1966. Two young couples were driving through a deserted arsenal about seven miles outside of Point Pleasant. The place was once known as the Virginia Ordinance Works, but it was locally called the "TNT Area."

Near one of the old power plants the four saw what looked

like a large pair of glowing red eyes staring at them. They dismissed them as belonging to some ordinary sort of animal. But a short time later they got a better view of "it." It was an undoubted monster—somewhat over six feet tall, and shaped generally like a man. But instead of arms it had gigantic wings "like an angel" according to one of the witnesses. It walked, or rather shuffled clumsily like a penguin. Then it spread its wings, which seemed to reach ten feet from tip to tip, and rose straight up like a helicopter.

That was more than enough for the young witnesses. They turned their car around and headed back to town just as fast as they could—about 100 m.p.h. Even at that speed the monster pursued them. Said the driver: "No matter how fast I went, it kept gliding over the roof, sort of moving from side to side. We could hear a flapping noise." It even seemed to attack, swooping down on the car and making a squealing noise "like a mouse."

By the time they had reached the city limits the creature had abandoned the chase. The four witnesses drove directly to the police station, where they reported the incident. The next morning the police dutifully investigated the TNT area, but found nothing except a few indeterminate indentations in the ground.

Shaken as they had been after their nighttime chase by the winged monster, the four young people had recovered sufficiently to be able to hold a small press conference the following morning in the county courthouse. The story created a minor sensation in the West Virginia papers, and local stringers passed the news on to the wire services. Some monster stories seem to make no publicity splash at all, but the strange happenings at the Point Pleasant TNT Area received a surprising amount of national attention. Soon television and radio crews visited the scene of the sighting.

In the beginning people referred to the "thing" simply as

"the Bird" or "the Big Bird." But shortly someone coined a catchy name which helped catapult the creature to a degree of national prominence. The thing at Point Pleasant was called Mothman. Batman was big on television at the time. Birdman would probably have been a more appropriate name, but it lacks the correct tone.

Mothman was reported to have appeared again and again. But there is little agreement as to just how many people saw him. Some newspaper and magazine articles have claimed that the flying monster was seen by hundreds of persons in the area over the next few months. Yet local police recorded only about a dozen reports of sightings. Investigators like John Keel counter by saying the police records are not at all adequate, because most people simply did not report the sightings to the police. Why should they? It wouldn't do any good, and, after all, it was no crime to see Mothman, or for that matter to be Mothman. Others did not wish to make their sightings public because they feared the ridicule that resulted from publicity. Keel also vaguely hinted that there might be other, deeper, and more important reasons why people were keeping quiet. Only after months of intensive investigation, he said, was he able to ferret out stories from some of the witnesses.

It was perfectly true that anyone who reported seeing Mothman was likely to face a good deal of ridicule. All the Mothman publicity had presented local teen-agers with a welcome diversion as well as an unparalleled opportunity for practical joking. The deserted TNT Area had always been a hangout for the kids anyway. It was a place where they went to drink and make love. Now there was a new sport, driving around the TNT Area with your horn blaring to see if you could flush out Mothman. An even more adventurous activity was putting on a sheet and standing by the roadside flapping your arms to see if you could frighten someone driving by. Noise from the TNT Area got so loud that people who lived in the vicinity had to call the police to restore quiet.

All the Mothman-sighting accounts collected by Keel and others follow the same general pattern. No one who went out deliberately looking for the monster ever saw it. Mothman's appearances always came as a surprise. As in the first sighting, the creature was usually standing by the side of the road. Then it spread its wings and flew straight up. Often it pursued the witnesses when they drove away. The descriptions were also similar—"like a big gray bird, with bright red eyes."

Only one witness, an eighteen-year-old girl, claimed to get a close look at Mothman's face, and her description is not terribly helpful: "It was horrible . . . like something out of a science fiction movie." She claimed that the eyes had a sort of hypnotic power. "Those eyes. They were a fiery red and once they were fixed on me I couldn't take my own eyes off them."

This particular witness also reported that after the encounter with Mothman her eyes burned for days. Other people reported trouble with their automobile ignitions and strange interference on radios and television sets in areas around Mothman sightings. Both of these phenomena, eye irritation and apparent electrical interference, have often been associated with UFO sightings. Thus another link between Mothman and the flying saucers was forged.

For his diligent Mothman research Keel was awarded the first "Ufologist of the Year" award at the Congress of Scientific Ufologists held in New York City in June 1967.

About a year after Mothman made his first appearance, Point Pleasant was again in the national news. A bridge that spanned the Ohio River near the town collapsed killing forty-four persons. It was the greatest United States bridge disaster in recent years. Could this be mere coincidence?

whispered the Mothman supporters. One theory was that the vibrations of the monster's great wings had caused the bridge to collapse. This theory was so farfetched that it gained few supporters even on the fringe. But many could still not shake the belief that Mothman was somehow connected with the bridge collapse. Perhaps he was an omen of evil. In medieval times people often associated catastrophes with the reported appearance of a dragon or sea serpent.

After the first reports of Mothman, some scientists tried to offer down-to-earth explanations of what the thing might be. Dr. Robert Smith of the West Virginia University biology department said that the creature might in reality be a rare sandhill crane. This bird may stand nearly six feet tall, and has red patches around its eyes. Others suggested that Mothman might be a misplaced snowy owl or just about any other large bird, whose size had been exaggerated beyond all reasonable bounds by frightened and excitable young people. The problem with any of the big bird theories is that the TNT Area is located adjacent to the Clifton F. McClintic Wildlife Station, and none of the rangers or other personnel at the Wildlife Station had seen any unusual birds during the time of the Mothman scare. They regarded all the big bird stories as just plain crazy.

The rangers at the Wildlife Station were not alone in their opinion. Despite stories to the contrary, the Point Pleasant police did not take the Mothman tales very seriously. They openly deprecated the reliability of the original witnesses. People who lived near the TNT Area had also never seen anything of Mothman, and were more annoyed by the teenagers than frightened by the thought of the monster flying overhead.

In 1968 when a group of flying saucer buffs went down to West Virginia from New York to investigate they were deeply disappointed by what they found, or rather by what they failed to find. One of them, Mark A. Samwick, summed up his feelings this way: "I did not go down to Point Pleasant with a negative attitude. I really hoped to find something concrete; but from this investigation I've found that the whole story falls flat on its face."

So after a brief sojourn in the light of publicity, Mothman has flapped off into limbo, without even a ballad to mark his passing. He will, of course, be back. He is now firmly entrenched in the occult underground's mythology, despite the doubts of the more reasonable buffs. The next time there is a monster scare in that part of the country the happenings at Point Pleasant will be retold.

The case of the Flatwoods monster and Mothman, because they have been fairly well investigated and documented, give us a close-up view of how a monster myth might begin. While in medieval times a dragon or other monster was identified as a creature from hell, today our monsters are often called creatures from outer space. But they too quickly acquire supernatural associations, such as the ability to knock down large bridges. The explanations for monsters may differ, but for many persons, thought processes have changed hardly at all for thousands of years.

Unsupported and almost silly, the Flatwoods monster and Mothman stories are doubtless just as reliable as many monster stories of the past or that supposedly come from distant places. Up close the flaws just become more obvious.

There is certainly no justification for general scoffing and merriment at the expense of those who took or still take these two monsters from space seriously. Both West Virginia monsters quickly became public jokes. Those who wished to spread the doctrine of Mothman were given rough treatment on some of the more impolite TV interview shows. The subject could hardly be mentioned in the press without a string of snide comments. In the end Mothman got much of his favorable publicity from sensational men's magazines and the publications put out by and for saucer buffs.

At the very same time, people who were writing equally improbable and unsupportable stories were received as respected guests on the biggest network TV interview shows. These stories were played up by national magazines and made the subject of best-selling books. Very few interviewers publicly insulted writers like John Fuller and Frank Edwards though they were writing essentially the same sort of invasion from space material. With a little luck, and perhaps better publicists, the happenings at Point Pleasant could have become as famous and been treated as seriously as the UFO sightings at Exeter, New Hampshire, in 1965. These sightings, if you will recall, sparked a whole new flying saucer "flap."

Of course, the idea of monsters from space did not originate with the flying saucer mania. People began worrying about flying saucers in 1947, but well before that, on October 30, 1938, Orson Welles adapted a story by H. G. Wells and used it as the basis for his now famous "War of the Worlds" broadcast. In the program Welles and his Mercury players dramatically described the invasion of earth by monsters from Mars. The program was done just as though it were a news broadcast covering a real invasion. Despite announcements that the program was really fiction a very large number of people throughout the country believed that they were actually listening to live news coverage of the beginning of the end for earth. They did what any normal person would do if faced with the announcement of an invasion of evil and powerful space monsters—they panicked.

Bug-eyed monsters (or BEMs as they were affectionately called) were a virtual fixture of pulp science fiction. In the years that followed World War II hardly a month went by without the newsstands being adorned with at least one magazine featuring a cover in which a spidery space creature was menacing a semi-nude girl. Earlier the seemingly endless series of Flash Gordon serials had their share of space monsters as did the Flash Gordon and Buck Rogers comics.

With all of this publicity as background it is rather surprising that the flying saucer mania did not produce more monster stories. There were plenty of reported landings and meetings and other sorts of contacts with the space people. Opinion was sharply divided as to whether these space people were good and out to help us or bad and out to get us. At a typical meeting of a flying saucer group one might hear views from "contactees" which ranged from Pollyanna to paranoia. But there was relatively little disagreement over what the space people looked like—they looked like us. Oh, some of them might be very tall or very short, or have funny eyes, but basically they were human in appearance, and usually indistinguishable from earthmen. From white earthmen, I might add. Occasionally shaved monkeys have been touted as the bodies of "little men" from space. While such manufactured monsters were popular a few hundred years ago, they get little attention today since most everyone knows what a monkey looks like, shaved or not.

It is a little difficult to decide whether the conformity in the description of the space people is due to a natural tendency on the part of all men to create gods and devils in their own image, or whether it was simply the result of a failure of imagination on the part of those who claimed to have contacted the space people.

Certainly there is no logical reason to believe that intelligent beings from other planets would look just like us. Indeed, there are rather good reasons for believing that they would not look at all like us. Different conditions on different planets would call for a host of different adaptations. And even if these theoretical space people came from a planet where the conditions almost exactly matched those on earth, why should they look like us? We are, after all, not the best of all possible end products of evolution.

A few years back some scientists speculated on possible shapes for space people. One idea was that a very serviceable form would be that of the mythical centaur. The four-legged stance would allow such a creature great power in running and walking. Our space centaur would also avoid the many back troubles which seem to be the inevitable result of our own upright posture. On the other hand, this centaur creature would have a pair of hands free for grasping and manipulating tools. If you think about it for a while, you may begin to wonder why the earth was not populated with such creatures.

So if and when we are visited by beings from another world, we must be prepared that their shape might look monstrous to us as ours almost surely will to them.

If and when . . . Do these visits lie only in a possible future, or could we have been visited by monsters from space in the past? As we have seen, the stories that come from the era of flying saucers do not inspire much confidence. But perhaps we have been visited some time before, long before, in a day when history and myth were one, and any such extraterrestrial contact would be passed on as a myth, and thus be completely misunderstood by future generations.

The science fiction writer Arthur C. Clarke once wrote a story in which the extraterrestrials who contacted earth early in man's history were horned creatures with leathern wings, and thus became the foundation for later devil myths.

Others have very seriously suggested that some of the events in the Bible, the destruction of Sodom and Gomorrah, for example, were actually the result of contact with a high extraterrestrial civilization. Fairly violent contact it must be noted. Curiously, very similar theories along this line have been advanced by atheists who are trying to prove that everything in the Bible can be explained by natural causes and those who hold fundamentalist beliefs and hold that all the Biblical events are literally true.

Various bits of material evidence for ancient extraterrestrial contact have been cited, but they are not impressive. The supposed drawings of spacemen found in caves in the Sahara have turned out to be drawings of men in ritual masks. Other ancient "extraterrestrial" artifacts have likewise been revealed as the results of misinterpretation or deliberate fraud.

Probably the most intriguing speculation regarding extraterrestrial contact put forward in recent years is that of the Harvard astronomer Dr. Carl Sagan. Dr. Sagan's theory concerns us here because the possible extraterrestrial creature has two heads, the body of a fish, and a pair of legs—it is truly monstrous in appearance. The speculation is about a legend which in Dr. Sagan's opinion "more nearly fulfills some of our criteria for a genuine contact myth."

The legend itself can only be accurately traced back to the time of Alexander the Great (356–323 B.C.) and to a Babylonian priest named Berosus. But if authentic, the myth itself deals with the very beginnings of civilization. It must be assumed that Berosus had access to documents dating back well before his own time and perhaps to documents far older than any which now survive. The first intriguing element in the story is that it indicates that civilization began in Mesopotamia, an area of the Middle East once inhabited by the Sumerians. The Sumerians, as far as anyone has been able to determine, were the first civilized people.

The origins of Sumerian civilization are obscure to us. As far as archaeologists have been able to determine, Sumerian civilization appeared almost fully formed in Mesopotamia sometime during the fourth mellennium B.C. According to all reputable theories of culture, civilizations do not just spring up fully formed. The Sumerians must have gone through a long stage of development elsewhere, and then migrated to Mesopotamia. But as to where they came from we haven't a clue.

Another possibility is that Sumerian civilization began under the influence of another high civilization. But there is no trace of this hypothetical master civilization. It is almost as if the skills of civilization were transmitted to the Sumerians by creatures from outer space, which brings us to our contact legend. The version that is available to us was set down in classical times by Alexander Polyhistor:

"Berosus, in his first book concerning the history of Babylonia [Babylonia became a general term to denote all Mesopotamian civilizations], informs us that he lived in the time of Alexander, the son of Philip. And he mentions that there were written accounts preserved at Babylon with the greatest care, comprehending a term of fifteen myriads of years. These writings contained a history of the heavens and the sea; of the birth of mankind; also of those who had sovereign rule; and of the actions achieved by them.

"And, in the first place, he described Babylonia as a country which lay between the Tigris and Euphrates. He mentions that it abounded with wheat, barley ocrus, sesamum; and in the lakes were found roots called gongage, which were good to be eaten, and were, in respect to nutriment, like barley. There were also palm trees and apples, and most kinds of fruits; fish, too, and birds; both those which are merely of flight, and those which take to the element of water. The part of Babylon which bordered upon Arabia was barren, and without water; but that which lay on the other side had hills, and was fruitful. At Babylon there was (in these times)a great resort of people of various nations, who inhabited Chaldea, and lived without rule and order, like the beasts of the field.

"In the first year there made its appearance, from a part of the Persian Gulf which bordered upon Babylonia, an animal endowed with reason, who was called Oannes. (According to the account of Apollodorus) the whole body of the animal was like that of a fish; and had under a fish's head another head, and also feet below, similar to those of a man, subjoined to the fish's tail. His voice, too, and language was articulate and human; and a representation of him is preserved even to this day [a representation still exists on an Assyrian cylinder seal].

"This Being, in the day-time used to converse with men; but took no food at that season; and he gave them an insight into letters, and sciences, and every kind of art. He taught them to construct houses, to found temples, to compile laws, and explained to them the principles of geometrical knowledge. He made them distinguish the seeds of the earth, and showed them how to collect fruits. In short, he instructed them in everything which could tend to soften manners and humanize mankind. From that time, so universal were his instructions, nothing material has been added by way of improvement. When the sun set it was the custom of this Being to plunge again into the sea, and abide all night in the deep; for he was amphibious.

"After this, there appeared other animals, like Oannes, of which Berosus promises to give an account when he comes to the history of kings. Moreover, Berosus wrote concerning the generation of mankind; of their different ways of life and of their civil policy . . ."

Other fragments based on Berosus' history have creatures like Oannes ruling the people of Mesopotamia, each having what seems to be an incredibly long reign. These creatures, known collectively as the Apkallu, are always described as "animals," "beings," "semi-daemons," and "personages" but never, significantly enough, as gods, although the Babylonians certainly worshipped plenty of strange-looking gods. In other fragments we find statements like "double-shaped personages came out of the sea to land," "the shape of a fish blended with that of a man," and "the same complicated form, between fish and man."

Dr. Sagan is impressed, and rightly so, by the straightforward, almost dry way in which these accounts are written. If one accepts the existence of the super-intelligent fish-man, the rest of the story has no obvious supernatural elements. It reads like the story of a highly civilized being bringing the fruits of civilization to the "natives."

Dr. Sagan finds another hint of extraterrestrial contact in some of the ancient Mesopotamian cylinder seals. In one of these there is what appears to be a sun or star. But surrounding the star are a number of other objects. "It is at least a natural assumption that they represent planets," writes Dr. Sagan. "But the idea of planets circling suns and stars is an idea which essentially originated with Copernicus—although some earlier speculations along these lines were mentioned in ancient Greece."

Now none of this "proves" that the Sumerians were contacted by intelligent fish-men from outer space. It would be utterly foolish to believe that this sort of evidence, which is open to a host of wildly different interpretations, could ever prove anything of the sort. Dr. Sagan is well aware of the limitations. "These cylinder seals may be nothing more than the experiments of the ancient unconscious mind to understand and portray a sometimes incomprehensible, sometimes hostile environment. The stories of the Apkallu may have been made out of whole cloth, perhaps as late as Babylonian times, perhaps by Berosus himself. Sumerian society may have developed gradually over many thousands of years."

However, he concludes, "Stories like the Oannes legend, and representations especially of the earliest civilizations on the Earth, deserve much more critical studies than have been performed heretofore, with the possibility of direct contact with an extraterrestrial civilization as one of many possible alternative interpretations."

As we have noted, the people of Mesopotamia, from the Sumerians on down, were exceptionally adept at creating creatures of monstrous shape and aspect. Now after a long journey into the history of monsters, in which we have found so many disappointingly unreal, it might not be out of line to speculate on the possibility that at least some of these very early monsters were real.

The earliest of human artists were quite realistic, faithfully portraying animals that they had seen with their own eyes. But when we come to the Sumerians and other civilized peoples we are suddenly confronted with creatures that display a bewildering jumble of characteristics. What caused this rather dramatic change in outlook? We might speculate that at least some of these monstrous creations were attempts at realistic interpretations of something that walked, crawled, flipped, flopped, floated, slithered, or oozed out of a space ship.

The composite of characteristics is easy to explain. A man, confronted with a creature the like of which he had never seen before, would be forced to attempt to describe it in familiar terms. Thus a creature like the Apkallu might have originally been described as having a body something like that of a fish. Later storytellers and artists would have passed on this description in a very literal way. There exists not a scrap of material proof to back up this theory. But still it is rather stimulating to think that those most fantastically conceived monsters of the ancients were not simply products of a primitive imagination.

Bibliography

Bibliography

The amount of literature concerning monsters of antiquity is staggering, and the works often repeat one another. Much of the current information concerning monsters is buried in the obscure journals of the monster buffs or in sensational men's magazines. Neither of these classes of publication reach the shelves of the average library. What follows is a selected list of books that the general reader might find interesting and available.

Barker, Gray. *They Knew Too Much About Flying Saucers*. New York: University Books, 1956.

Bernheimer, Richard. *Wild Men in the Middle Ages*. Cambridge: Harvard University Press, 1952.

Burton, Maurice. *Animal Legends*. New York: Coward McCann, 1957.

——. *The Elusive Monster*. London: Rupert-Hart-Davis, 1961.

Carrington, Richard A. *Elephants*. New York: Basic Books, 1959.

——. *A Guide to Earth History*. London: Chatto & Windus, 1956.

——. *Mermaids and Mastodons*. New York: Rinehart & Co., 1957.

Cohen, Daniel. *The Age of Giant Mammals*. New York: Dodd, Mead & Co., 1969.

——. *Myths of the Space Age*. New York: Dodd, Mead & Co., 1967.

Colbert, Edwin H. *The Age of Reptiles*. New York: W.W. Norton Co., 1965.

——. *Dinosaurs: Their Discovery and Their World*. New York: E.P. Dutton & Co., 1961.

——. *Evolution of the Vertebrates*. New York: John Wiley & Sons, 1955.

——. *Men and Dinosaurs*. New York: E.P. Dutton & Co., 1968.

Coon, Carleton S. *The Origin of Races*. New York: Alfred A. Knopf, 1968.

De Camp, L. Sprague and Catherine. *Ancient Ruins and Archaeology*. New York: Doubleday & Co., 1964.

——. *The Day of the Dinosaur*. New York: Doubleday & Co., 1968.

Dinsdale, Tim. *The Leviathans*. London: Routledge & Kegan Paul, 1966.

——. *The Loch Ness Monster*. Philadelphia: Chilton Books, 1961.

Edwards, Frank. *Stranger Than Science*. New York: Lyle Stuart, 1959.

——. *Strangest of All*. New York: Lyle Stuart, 1956.

Fort, Charles. *The Books of Charles Fort*. New York: Published for the Fortean Society by Henry Holt & Co., 1941.

Gardner, Martin. *Fads and Fallacies in the Name of Science*. New York: Dover Publications, 1957.

Goodavage, Joseph F. *Astrology: The Space Age Science*. West Nyack, N.Y.: Parker Publishing Co., 1966.

Goodrich, Norma Lorre. *The Medieval Myths*. New York: Mentor Books, 1961.

Gould, Rupert T. *The Case for the Sea Serpent*. London: Allan, 1930.

——. *Enigmas*. New York: University Books, 1961.

——. *The Loch Ness Monster and Others*. London: Geoffrey Bles, 1934.

——. *Oddities*. New York: University Books, 1965.

Green, John. *On the Track of the Sasquatch*. Agassiz, British Columbia: Cheam Publishing Co., 1968.

Hawkins, Thomas. *The Book of the Great Sea Dragons, Icthyosauri and Plesiosauri*. London: William Pickering, 1840.

Helm, Thomas. *Monsters of the Deep*. New York: Dodd, Mead & Co., 1962.

Heuvelmans, Bernard. *In The Wake of the Sea Serpents*. New York: Hill & Wang, 1968.

——. *On the Tracks of Unknown Animals.* New York: Hill & Wang, 1959.

Hill, Douglas and Williams, Pat. *The Supernatural.* New York: Hawthorn Books, 1966.

Hillary, Sir Edmund and Doig, Desmond. *High in the Thin Cold Air.* New York: Doubleday & Co., 1962.

Holiday, F.W. *The Great Orm of Loch Ness.* New York: W.W. Norton & Co., 1969.

Hurwood, Bernhardt J. *Vampires, Werewolves and Ghouls.* New York: Ace Books, 1968.

Ingersoll, Ernest. *Dragons and Dragon Lore.* New York: Payson & Clarke, 1928.

Keel, John. *Jadoo.* New York: Julian Messner, 1957.

Larousse Encyclopedia of Mythology. London: Paul Hamlyn, 1959.

Lewinsohn, Richard. *Animals, Men and Myths.* New York: Harper & Brothers, 1954.

Ley, Willy. *Another Look at Atlantis and Fifteen Other Essays.* New York: Doubleday & Co., 1960.

——. *The Dawn of Zoology.* Englewood Cliffs, N.J.: Prentice-Hall, 1968.

——. *Dragons in Amber.* New York: The Viking Press, 1951.

——. *Exotic Zoology.* New York: The Viking Press, 1959.

——. *The Lungfish and the Unicorn.* New York: Modern Age, 1941.

Lum Peter. *Fabulous Beasts.* London: Thames & Hudson, 1951.

MacDougall, Curtis D. *Hoaxes.* New York: Dover Publications, 1958.

Mackay, Charles. *Extraordinary Popular Delusions and the Madness of Crowds.* Boston: L.C. Page & Co., 1932.

Mandeville, Sir John. *The Travels of Sir John Mandeville with Three Narratives in Illustration of It,* ed. A.W. Pollard. New York: Dover Publications. 1964.

Martin, P.S. and Wright, H.E., editors. *Pleistocene Extinctions, the Search for a Cause.* New Haven: Yale University Press, 1967.

Norman, Eric. *The Abominable Snowman.* New York: Award Books, 1969.

Patterson, Roger. *Do Abominable Snowmen of America Really Exist?* Yakima, Washington: Trailblazer Research, 1966.

Polo, Marco. *The Travels of Marco Polo,* translated and edited by Sir Henry Yaile. London: Murray, 1921.

Rampa, T. Lobsang. *The Third Eye.* New York: Ballantine Books, 1964.

Randall, Richard N., editor. *A Cloisters Bestiary.* New York: The Metropolitan Museum of Art, 1960.

Romer, Alfred S. *Vertebrate Paleontology.* Chicago: University of Chicago Press, 1945.

Sagen, Carl and Shklovskii, I.S. *Intelligent Life in the Universe.* San Francisco: Holden-Day, 1966.

Sanderson, Ivan T. *Abominable Snowmen, Legend Come to Life.* Philadelphia: Chilton Books, 1961.

———. *Uninvited Visitors. A Biologist Looks at UFOs.* New York: Cowles Educational Corp., 1967.

Schaller, George B. *The Year of the Gorilla.* Chicago: University of Chicago Press, 1964.

Silverberg, Robert. *Scientists and Scoundrels.* New York: Thomas Y. Crowell Co., 1965.

Simpson, George Gaylord. *Life of the Past.* New Haven: Yale University Press, 1961.

———. *The Meaning of Evolution.* New Haven: Yale University Press, 1949.

Soule, Gardner. *Trail of the Abominable Snowman.* New York: G.P. Putnam's Sons, 1966.

———. *The Maybe Monsters.* New York: G.P. Putnam's Sons, 1963.

Spence, Lewis. *Encylopedia of Occultism.* New York: University Books, 1960.

Steiger, Brad. *Strangers from the Skies.* New York: Award Books, 1966.

Sullivan, Walter. *We Are Not Alone.* New York: McGraw-Hill Book Co., 1964.

Ullman, James Ramsey. *The Age of Mountaineering.* Philadelphia: J.B. Lippincott Co., 1941.

———. *Tiger of the Snows.* New York: G.P. Putnam's Sons, 1955.

Walker, Ernest P. and Associates. *Mammals of the World* (two volumes). Baltimore: The Johns Hopkins Press, 1964.

Wendt, Herbert. *Before the Deluge.* New York: Doubleday & Co., 1968.

———. *Out of Noah's Ark.* London: Weidenfeld & Nicholson, 1959.

Whyte, C. *More Than a Legend.* London: Hamish Hamilton, 1957.

Index

Index